THE SCHOOL FOR LIES

THE SCHOOL FOR LIES

A PLAY ADAPTED FROM
MOLIÈRE'S *LE MISANTHROPE*

DAVID IVES

NORTHWESTERN UNIVERSITY PRESS
EVANSTON, ILLINOIS

Northwestern University Press
www.nupress.northwestern.edu

Printed in the United States of America

10 9 8 7 6 5 4 3 2 1

LIBRARY OF CONGRESS
CATALOGING-IN-PUBLICATION DATA

Ives, David.
    The school for lies : a play adapted from Moliere's Le misanthrope / David Ives.
        p. cm.
    "The School for Lies, an adaptation of Moliere's Le Misanthrope, received its world premiere at Classic Stage Company in New York City (Brian Kulick, artistic director; Jessica R. Jenen, executive director; Jeff Griffin, general manager) on April 28, 2011."
    ISBN 978-0-8101-2882-8 (pbk. : alk. paper)
    1. France—Social life and customs—17th century—Drama. 2. Man-woman relationships—Drama. 3. Molière, 1622–1673—Adaptations. I. Molière, 1622–1673. Misanthrope. II. Title.
PS3559.V435S36 2012
812.54—dc23

                                2012022494

♾ The paper used in this publication meets the minimum requirements of the American National Standard for Information Sciences—Permanence of Paper for Printed Library Materials, ANSI Z39.48-1992.

This play is for Martha,
naturellement.

CONTENTS

PRODUCTION HISTORY

The School for Lies, an adaptation of Molière's *Le Misanthrope,* received its world premiere at Classic Stage Company in New York City (Brian Kulick, artistic director; Jessica R. Jenen, executive director; Jeff Griffin, general manager) on April 28, 2011. The director was Walter Bobbie; the set designer, John Lee Beatty; the costume designer, Anita Yavich; the lighting designer, Peter Kaczorowski; and the sound design was by Acme Sound Partners. The production manager was Production Core; the production stage manager was Terri K. Kohler, and the assistant stage manager was Lauren Kurinskas. The cast was as follows:

Frank	Hamish Linklater
Celimene	Mamie Gummer
Eliante	Jenn Gambatese
Philinte	Hoon Lee
Arsinoé	Alison Fraser
Clitander	Frank Harts
Oronte	Rick Holmes
Acaste	Matthew Maher
Dubois/Basque	Steven Boyer

THE SCHOOL FOR LIES

CHARACTERS

Frank, a native of Paris, newly returned
Celimene, a young widow of Paris society
Eliante, her cousin
Philinte, enamored of Eliante
Arsinoé, a moral pillar
Clitander, an influential courtier
Oronte, a boulevard bard
Acaste, a moneyed marquis
Dubois, Celimene's servant ⎫ played by
Basque, Frank's valet ⎭ the same actor

THE SETTING

Celimene's drawing room. Paris, 1666.

PRONUNCIATIONS

Celimene:	Selly-*menn* [rhymes with "many men"]
Eliante:	Eh-*lyahnt* [rhymes with "want"]
Philinte:	Fee-*lant* [rhymes with "can't"]
Arsinoé:	Ar-*sin*-oh-eh [rhymes with "in a way"]
Clitander:	Cluh-*tann*-dur [rhymes with "meander"]
Oronte:	Or-*ahnt* [rhymes with "dilettante"]
Acaste:	A-*kast* [rhymes with "aghast"]
Damis:	Dah-*mee* [rhymes with "ah me"]
Dubois:	Dyoo-*bwah*
Basque:	Bask
Alceste:	Al-*sesst*

Note: For metrical purposes, "Madame" with an "e" is pronounced "muh*damm*," while "Madam" without an "e" is pronounced *madd*-um.

ACT 1

[CELIMENE's *drawing room. Paris, 1666. Morning. Some fashionable chairs, an elegant divan, and a desk with papers. At rise: the actor playing* PHILINTE *addresses the audience.*]

PHILINTE:
Monsieur Molière, unfortunately dead,
Sends fond regrets from his eternal bed.
For it was he with an immortal play
Who mixed the batter for tonight's soufflé
In 1666—his entertainment
Titled *The Misanthrope*. A dark arraignment
Of human life and love and hope, blah blah,
But funny, too, and I mean funny ha-ha.
A masterpiece from comedy's top mensch!
Too bad for us he left the play in French,
Which no one speaks—except, of course, the French,
And pompous types who bandy terms like *"genre."*
Is it a compliment, or does it honor a
Great work, to render it in our base tongue?

And then to "fix" a plot the angels sung?
Well, as I say, Molière has packed his tent
And our producers gave him two percent—
So screw Molière, we'll do our own damn version!
In English, thank you, for your full immersion,
That you may revel in our native tones—
At least those who (*hello?!*) turn off your phones.
Another sign of how the world has changed!
Can you believe, back then, what dunces ranged
In every level of society?
Or that buffoons of wild variety
Actually held positions of great power?
Thank God we've none of that! No fools to sour
Our peace, no hypocrites to etch in acid.
What use for satire, now our lives are placid
And all our ills are solved by techno-fix?
Let's pity, then, poor sixteen sixty-six.

[CLITANDER *enters. Like* PHILINTE, *he is colorfully and elaborately dressed.*]

CLITANDER:
Monsieur, monsieur, you really are too sweet.
At Madam Celimene's I always meet
The most enchanting, most delightful people—
A congregation of which you're the steeple,
You who in charm and elegance outdo
All men from France to distant Timbuktu!

PHILINTE:
But *you*, monsieur . . .

CLITANDER:
            No, *you* . . . Well, yes, it's true,
I dazzle Paris.

PHILINTE:
>You are a pinnacle!

CLITANDER:
But you . . .

PHILINTE:
>But you, sir—call me cynical—
You are *Polaris*!

CLITANDER:
>Perhaps. But time is short.
Our hostess's lawsuit wants help at court.
I'm off to spread my little patch of clover
But I'll return before the morning's over.

PHILINTE:
Oh, good. You'll get to meet my newest friend.
He's late, but has a talent to offend.

CLITANDER:
A friend of yours, monsieur? Call me pre-smitten.

PHILINTE:
A Frenchman born, Frank's been some years in Britain
Where he's picked up (I swear it's not a front)
A preternatural gift for being blunt.
Frank's so determined to be fully candid
His every syllable can seem backhanded.

CLITANDER:
Opinionated, then?

PHILINTE:
>Invincible.
He'll pillory people just on principle.
I know there're those who'd say that he's a crank.
I find him fun. A modern mountebank.

FRANK [*from offstage*]:
No, I will NOT, the answer's NO, you blank,
You frog-faced fop, you perfumated plank,
You cringing idiot!

PHILINTE:
                    Ah. That sounds like Frank.

[FRANK *enters. He is dressed all in unornamented black and carries a severe black hat.* DUBOIS *follows.*]

FRANK:
Leave me alone, leave me alone, God damn it!
Will you piss off, or do I have to ram it . . .
Can you believe this lackey stooge, this brat,
This doormat wanted me to leave my hat?

PHILINTE:
Frank, there's a gentleman right here who's curious . . .

FRANK:
Will you excuse me, please? I'm being furious.
As if I'd want to stick around this dump!
Whose clientele no doubt is from the sump pump
Of all that's trumped up, dull, and artificial.
Where even the artifice is artificial.
Where what's official is a fishy smell.
Fine, take it, then!

[FRANK *flings his hat at* DUBOIS, *who exits with it.*]

                    Go hang it up in hell!

CLITANDER:
Monsieur, this gentleman has sung the heady
Abundance of your character. Already—

Although we're total strangers—I've conceived
Such high esteem for you I would be grieved,
No, desolate, what gentleman could bear it
If I did not acknowledge your vast merit,
If I did not, here, instantly extend
My offer—no, my *plea*—to call you "friend."

FRANK:
What?

CLITANDER:
I note your widow's weeds. Was it a wife?

FRANK:
No, I wear black in mourning for your life.

CLITANDER:
A pithy joke. You live up to the rumor.

FRANK:
I never joke. I have no sense of humor.

CLITANDER:
Monsieur . . .

FRANK:
        Just Frank.

CLITANDER:
            But you're still French.

FRANK:
                     Alas.

CLITANDER:
François, I'll call you.

FRANK:
        Stuff it up your class.

CLITANDER:
You really have no inhibitions, do you?
Well, I have influence. Should someone sue you,
Please, call on me for help. Don't be embarrassed.

FRANK:
Who'd want to sue me?

CLITANDER:
                              Sir, they're suing all Paris!
There's not a man or woman not in court
For slander. This town teems!

FRANK:
                              With sewers?

CLITANDER:
                                             With tort.
It's why I'm here. Our hostess, to her sorrow,
Will come to judgment with a case tomorrow
And wants my help to, let's say, *sway* the bench?
You've met our Celimene? A glorious wench.
A widow, sir, of beauty and such spirit,
A wit so sharp no suitor dare come near it.
Although God knows we try, ha ha.

FRANK:
                              Ha ha.

CLITANDER:
The way she makes us *vie*, ha ha.

FRANK:
                              Ha ha.

CLITANDER:
So you'll accept my friendship, freely proffered?

FRANK:
Monsieur, the gift's too great. The precious offer
Of your acquaintance, your fraternity
Extended to a tetchy wretch like me?
What if we differ? Friends are not exempt.
And having bickered, dipped into contempt,
We'd slip from difference to dislike to tension,
To hatred, thence to scorn, by this declension
Into a state (I say it with a gulp)
Where I'd be forced to mash you into pulp.
And yet you'd thrust your friendship on me, will you?
No, save yourself, sir, please! Don't make me kill you.

CLITANDER [*to* PHILINTE]:
My friend, your friend's a prodigy indeed.
This man's a miracle!

PHILINTE:
                              Sir, *you* exceed
As prodigy all other men in Paris.
You are a peak, a Himalayan terrace
To which we humble mortals have no claim.

CLITANDER:
You are the Western world's eternal flame!

PHILINTE:
But *you* . . .

CLITANDER:
             No, *you* . . .

PHILINTE:
                              Your servant, sir.

CLITANDER:
                                           The same.

[*They embrace, and* CLITANDER *exits.*]

FRANK:
Who's the jerk?

PHILINTE:
                    Not a clue. Oh, yes. Clitander.

FRANK:
Leave me.

PHILINTE:
          What?

FRANK:
                    I said *leave me.*

PHILINTE:
                              Why?

FRANK:
                                        In candor,
If you're of his mind, then you're not of *my* kind.
Leave me, or *I* shall leave!

PHILINTE:
                    Frank, what's the matter?

FRANK:
You truckle to this pompous tit, you flatter,
You fall upon him like some long-lost wife,
(*But YOU, monsieur! No, YOU!*) your words so rife
With passion and your ecstasies so wild
I half-expected you'd produce a child.
And then (I wonder you don't die of shame)
You tell me you don't know this asshole's *name*?

PHILINTE:
What's *your* prescription? Heap him with abuse?

FRANK:
Or—be proactive. Buy yourself a noose.

PHILINTE:
Politeness hardly warrants self-destruction.

FRANK:
Polite? When you two hugged I could hear *suction.*

PHILINTE:
Seriously, Frank. What would you have me do?

FRANK:
Speak from your soul. Say nothing that's not true.
And Number One among the things that bug me?
Don't ever, ever, ever, *ever* hug me.

PHILINTE:
But in society . . .

FRANK:
                    "Society . . . !"

PHILINTE:
Which in return for manners gives its prize . . .

FRANK:
Society is nothing but a school for lies.
This city's built on them, and may it wilt on them.
Good-bye!

PHILINTE:
            But Frank . . .

FRANK:
                            How can a man abet
This two-faced pestilential *etiquette,*
The pretzeled pomp of pimping politesse
That masks indifference with a limp caress?

What's yours or mine or any friendship worth
If handed out to every douche on earth?
(Like him.) Love everyone and you love no one.
You're as promiscuous as a bedpan.

PHILINTE:

                              Go on.

FRANK:
I am not ANY man! No, pick me out,
Distinguish, honor me! Don't trick me out
With protestations of ersatz affection
While your true feelings lurk beneath detection.
Chastise me if you prize me! Slap my face!
Just don't confuse me with the human race.

[DUBOIS *has entered with a tray of hors d'oeuvres.*]

DUBOIS:
A canapé?

[PHILINTE *takes one.*]

PHILINTE:
                    The rules of mere decorum . . .

FRANK:
Spare me! The handbook for a cringing quorum
Of sterile, puerile, swan-eating, canary-
Sucking nonentities. What, I should vary
My identity to suit some mannequin
Whom simple truth would cause a panic in,
Who'd rather talk about the cannikin
Of fine Lafitte he drank last night, with whom?
The artisanal sushi he consumed?

PHILINTE:

You'd rather brood? Or snub him, and be rude?

DUBOIS:

A canapé, monsieur?

[FRANK *upends the canapé tray, sending them flying.*]

FRANK:

Give me real *FOOD*!
Some honest bread! Pure water! Musky plums
As might have purpled Caravaggio's thumbs!
I crave the prophet's diet—locusts and honey!

PHILINTE:

Frank, that's because you haven't any *money.*

FRANK:

Where are the great men of the Renaissance?
We spend our days discussing restaurants!
What shows we've seen! It being our highest attainment
To waste a lifetime viewing *entertainment.*
Tasteless commedias whose collective text
Could be our one-word national motto: *"NEXT!"*
Why not? Now *life's* a synonym for *leisure,*
Who cares if we have cultural amnesia?
Our daughters dress like whores, our sons are rude.
These kids can't scratch their own initials, dude!
And all our chat, our heliumated high-talk!
Fat fucks in flip-flops blocking up the sidewalk!
Each one upholding our most sacred law:
The people's right to suck a soda straw!
Dear God, this country agitates my bile.
The ignorance, the greed, the lust, it's vile.
Come down! Destroy us! Do your work and ravage!

PHILINTE:
You wouldn't say that this is rather . . .

FRANK:

                                               . . . savage?
Yes, why? You find it tedious? Boring? Dull?
To see the mask ripped from the human skull?

PHILINTE:
Dear Frank, you're so unique. You're so eccentric.

FRANK:
Eccentric? I, you stencil? I'm *authentic*!
The truest democrat on this earth's crust.
I treat all men with uniform disgust.

PHILINTE:
But why? The ignorant iniquity
Of Man dates back to the antiquity
Of Man. Your ravings won't change humankind.
What benefit in having underlined
Men's faults instead of understanding
Them?

FRANK:
    Eugh.

PHILINTE:
               Forgiving?

FRANK:
                       Eugh.

PHILINTE:
                            Not reprimanding
Them. *Loving* them.

FRANK:
              EUGH!

PHILINTE:

As Buddha would do.

FRANK:

Did Buddha know what barracuda do?

PHILINTE:

I know all earthly creatures have their failings.
Do you see me expostulating? Railing?
My equanimity is automatic.

FRANK:

What equanimity? You're just phlegmatic.

PHILINTE:

My phlegm's as philosophic as your spleen.

FRANK:

Will nothing make your phlegm begin to steam?

PHILINTE:

All right, we're wicked, selfish, two-faced, mean.
Yet I'm no more disgusted with my species
Than when I watch caged monkeys throwing feces.

FRANK:

And if a so-called "friend" told lies and threw some?
Traduced you? Started rumors?

PHILINTE:

God, you're gruesome.

FRANK:

No, no, if he or she, with some false tale
Disgraced you in an act of base betrayal?
You wouldn't view that once-fond friend with loathing?

[ORONTE *enters. He has a conspicuous wart on his nose.*]

ORONTE:
Good morning!

FRANK [*to* ORONTE, *pointing to* PHILINTE]:
        Sir, this man wears women's clothing.

PHILINTE:
Now really . . .

FRANK:
        He won't tell. He's shy that way.
I'm talking total dragster, by the way.

PHILINTE:
A little joke of Frank's.

FRANK:
        And here's the chaser:
He dresses up as Queen Marie-Theresa.

PHILINTE:
Ha, ha.

FRANK:
        The satin gear. The sky-blue gown.

PHILINTE:
Ha, ha.

FRANK:
        Tits out to here. A diamond crown.

PHILINTE:
What fun.

FRANK:
        Oh, he's a dream in dimity.

PHILINTE:
You note my perfect equanimity.

ORONTE:

I see now. You're Philinte's new friend François!

FRANK:

Just Frank.

ORONTE:

How you exude a je ne sais quoi!
May we embrace?

FRANK:

No.

[ORONTE *hugs* FRANK, *who stands stiffly unresponding.*]

PHILINTE:

Frank, this is Oronte.

ORONTE:

All day, François, I've had no greater want
Than meeting you. Don't praise me. You're too kind.
At Madam Celimene's I always find
Such open arms, such ready amity.
I hope that you won't think it vanity,
Or wouldn't mind, now that you're such a friend,
If I just share with you a poem I've penned . . .

[*He takes out a piece of paper.*]

PHILINTE:

Stop. *Stop.* Um, no. You wouldn't want to do that.

ORONTE:

Not read?

PHILINTE:

        I somehow sense that you might rue that.
The glare. The room. Noise from the boulevard . . .

ORONTE:

Frank might expect it, knowing I'm a bard.
That I'm . . . *Oronte*!

FRANK:

        Who?

ORONTE:

                Please, François, be hard
And tell me: should I publish this, or let it sink?

FRANK:

I must recuse myself. I have this kink.

ORONTE:

Which is . . . ?

FRANK:

        I'll tell you what I really think.
A word which, you may notice, rhymes with "stink."

ORONTE:

Thank God! Some candor in this lying age!
Before we met, I *knew* you were a sage.
Oh, pwease?

FRANK:

        All right.

ORONTE:

              Now don't you flatter, feign,
Equivocate, or gloss. I won't complain.
Just speak your thoughts. Don't palliate. Don't pander.

PHILINTE:

(Remember, Frank. We have penalties for slander.)

FRANK:
(What happens if I penalize his rhyme scheme?)

ORONTE:
Ready?

FRANK:
      Like bystanders at a crime scene.

ORONTE [*clears his throat elaborately, then*]:
"*Song.*" Colon. Formally the poem's a song,
You see.

[*He clears his throat again.*]

      "*Song.*"

FRANK:
           Colon.

ORONTE:
                  Thank you.

FRANK:
                          Is it long?

ORONTE:
Not very.

FRANK:
      Good.

ORONTE:
           It's just a simple thing.

FRANK:
That's understood.

ORONTE:
           My verses like to sing
With ancient fragrances, a whiff of Homer.

FRANK:
I thought I sniffed a primitive aroma.

ORONTE [*clears throat elaborately, then*]:
"*Song.*" Colon. "*Hope . . .*" An hour was all I gave it.

FRANK:
Sir, if it's shit then fifty years won't save it.
Proceed. We know the title. [*Clearing throat*] "*Hope.*"

ORONTE:
                              "*Ah, Phyllis . . . !*"
A pseudonym for *Her*, the amaryllis-
Like damsel I've indited this same song to.

FRANK:
Why don't you name the dame?

ORONTE:
                    It would be wrong to.

FRANK:
You can't address her? Why? Some legal hitch?

ORONTE:
She doesn't know I love.

FRANK:
                    So tell the bitch!

PHILINTE:
Well, I, for one, am utterly enthralled.
"*Ah, Phyllis!*" That tristesse. That dying fall.

FRANK:
Appalling.

PHILINTE:
            Gentlemen . . . ?

FRANK:

Yes, please!

ORONTE [*clears throat, then*]:

"*Ah, Phyllis . . . !*"

FRANK:
Of course, what idiot doesn't want to thrill us
With noodling proof of his poetic shtick?
"An Elegy To My Late Poodle's Dick."
I told a poet-friend the other day
About his so-called "art," I said, *Don't bray*
Your every rippling fart in limping distichs.
Taking a poop in public's not artistic.

ORONTE:
Are you implying that I'm wrong to write?

FRANK:
I didn't say that.

[ORONTE *clears his throat to go on, but . . .*]

I say one must fight
This hemorrhoidal itch to manufacture
Gibberish. If one's talentless, why fracture
The rules of poesy *and* your good name
In futile forays trying to conquer fame?
Why trade the moniker "Boronte" . . .

ORONTE:

Oronte.

FRANK:
. . . for that of ditty-maker, dilettante,
Publishing scoundrel, rhapsode of the odious?
"Boronte! Whose mediocrity's commodious!"

So *please* (I begged my friend) give up the race!
Abuse is staring you right in the face!
It sees your pimples and your filthy pores.
Would it ignore (all these are metaphors)
A massive honking purple wart, like yours?

ORONTE:
So I resemble him, your futile friend?

FRANK:
I didn't say that.

[ORONTE *clears his throat to go on, but . . .*]

          Why pick up a pen
When every word's an infelicity?
A tribute to inauthenticity?

[DUBOIS *has appeared with more canapés on his salver.*]

DUBOIS:
A canapé?

[FRANK *upends the salver, sending the canapés flying.*]

FRANK:
        GIVE ME *SIMPLICITY*!
Not painted bric-a-brac from some dull dope!
Forgive me, we were where? Yes, colon: "*Hope.*"

ORONTE:
"*Ah, Phyllis, Phyllis, Phyllis,*
  You're like some strange bacillus . . ."

FRANK:
"Bacillus"! *WHAT?!*

ORONTE:

Did I misuse the term?

FRANK:

How fresh, to rhyme one's girlfriend with a germ.

ORONTE:

"Ah, Phyllis, Phyllis, Phyllis,
  You're like some strange bacillus.
  Do you intend to kill us
  With gazes that can chill us
  And make us mope? O spill us
  A length of rope! Instill us,
  Fair maid, with . . ."

FRANK:

Hope?

ORONTE:

". . . with hope. Fulfill us,
O Phyllis, Phyllis . . ."

FRANK:

Phyllis.

ORONTE:

". . . Phyllis."
The End.

[PHILINTE *applauds.*]

PHILINTE:

It's brilliant! So well-made. So *sure.*

ORONTE:

For some pains, poetry's the only cure.
Applause, the poet's only earthly balm.
Not that I'd lure a compliment, a palm,

A puff, a kindly word, some sympathy . . .
No, I abjure all empty empathy,
Inured to being ignored for plying the pure.
What need for words like *brilliant, well-made, sure*?

[*To* FRANK]

Your weighty silence tokens . . . what, monsieur?

FRANK:
I'm thinking . . . *Virgil.*

ORONTE:
                    Virgil did inspire this.

FRANK:
But would Virgil link his lady to a virus?
Or segue from Miss Microbe to a rope,
Straining with feeble rhymes like *mope* and *hope*?

ORONTE:
My friend, you certainly are analytic.

FRANK:
I make my living as a drama critic.

ORONTE:
Well, I maintain this poem's rather good.

FRANK:
I'll just say this, monsieur, colon: *you would.*
Pardon if I don't duplicate your taste.

ORONTE:
Why, it's a little gem.

FRANK:
                    It's tinsel. Paste.
It's dull, derivative, pale, pompous, trite.

ORONTE:
This city's full of fans for what I write.

FRANK:
Yes, sycophants who're brown well past their noses.
You'd trust a fecophile to judge your roses?

ORONTE:
So you're the be-all end-all? You're the word?

FRANK:
Well, here's a word to think on, colon: *turd*.
Indeed, the next time you've a poem to set
I'd print it on perfumed *papier toilette*.

ORONTE:
You'll pay, sir, for that slanderous retort!

FRANK:
Fine. Utilize the cash to lose that wart.

ORONTE [*to* PHILINTE]:
You're his accomplice! I'll see you both in court!

FRANK:
Your servant, sir.

[ORONTE *exits.*]

Thank God we're rid of *him*.

PHILINTE:
But this is serious, Frank. No, this is grim.
You need a lawyer.

FRANK:
Why?

PHILINTE:

It's foolhardy
Not to hire one.

FRANK:

But I'm the injured party!
Injured by all his arty verbal sludge.
I should sue *him*.

PHILINTE:

But Frank . . .

FRANK:

Bring on the judge!

PHILINTE:
Who'll represent you?

FRANK:

Reason, Right, and Justice.

PHILINTE:
If they find *me* complicit . . .

FRANK:

Let them bust us!
I should be crucified before the throng
Because I wouldn't praise his putrid song?
And here's my evidence!

PHILINTE:

But they'll abuse it.
They'll massacre your case.

FRANK:

Fine. Then I'll lose it.

PHILINTE:
It's folly, Frank! Can't you for once be wise?

FRANK:

God help the man who is, in this world's eyes.

PHILINTE:

Well, please, behave yourself with Celimene.

FRANK:

Are you in love with this illustrious hen?
Why all the Sen-Sen, all the lubrication
Each time her name pops up in conversation?

PHILINTE:

I love her cousin—pure and kind Eliante.

FRANK:

Oh, Christ. Sounds like some simpering, pious aunt.

PHILINTE:

Eliante's the sun, I am her wandering planet.
I knew it instantly. Her eyes began it . . .

FRANK:

And she loves you?

PHILINTE:

                  Who knows? I haven't said.

FRANK:

Well, tell her then! "I love you!" Bang! To bed!

[CELIMENE enters, unnoticed by FRANK, accompanied by ELIANTE and
ACASTE. CELIMENE wears a bright and fashionable gown.]

I just can't comprehend your subtle set.
As for your hostess—sounds like a coquette.
One of these social magpies. Faddish, feigning,
Poised, predatory, but always "entertaining,"
With men on leashes panting for her twitch.
Your Celimene sounds like a royal b—

CELIMENE:

How I've *itched*
To meet you. Here you stand now, waxing wroth.
To my amazement, a man of the cloth!
Oh, bless me, father, I have sinned, and deeply.
Do say a Mass for us, but do it cheaply.
You see, I have this court case coming due.
This time tomorrow I'll not have a sou
Unless you've got some pull with [*points upward*] You-Know-Who.

[*No response.*]

Struck dumb, apparently. Well, here's Eliante,
Aglow with goodness, of which she's a font.
Philinte you know. Marquis Acaste, who's no one.

[*No response.*]

Should you experience an emotion, show one.
Philinte, will you uncork your minister?
His silence is becoming sinister.

FRANK:
'Tis not my suit of inky black, madame,
That can denote all that I mean, or am.
I have a darker purpose, past all showing.

CELIMENE:
Darker than this? So this is . . . easygoing?

FRANK:
Forgive me. I know somber tones aren't chic
Amongst the gaudier fashions of your cleeque.

CELIMENE:
In my "cleeque" one can be a humble baker.
I don't recall we've had an undertaker.

FRANK:
I'm an old friend of death.

CELIMENE:
                              Yes, evidently.
You mimic rigor mortis so intently.
Though corpses commonly don't seem to seethe.
Or is that you've just begun to teethe?

FRANK:
At least my clothes reflect my attitude.
Don't widows wear black, in the platitude?

CELIMENE:
Some do affect it, for custom or art.
I wear my widow's weeds inside my heart.

FRANK:
How noble. Or what rank enormity.

CELIMENE:
You, sir, prescribe to *me* conformity?

FRANK:
I like the plain. I'm simple as my sleeve.

CELIMENE:
Use it to wave good-bye and you can leave.
Or do we need a vat of holy chrism
And someone to perform an exorcism?
Some Chinese yang to counteract your yin?

FRANK [*grimly*]:
I'm having fun.

CELIMENE:
                    Well, that explains the grin.

[CLITANDER *enters.*]

But here's a dispatch from the vale of sin.
Philinte has brought a friend to entertain us.
He's got the comic kick of Coriolanus.

CLITANDER:
Yes, I've already friended dear François.

FRANK:
Then I foe'd him and fee-fi-fo faux pas.

CELIMENE:
So is there gossip?

CLITANDER:
                    Oh, there is.

CELIMENE:
                              Fess up.

[CLITANDER *whispers in her ear.*]

You're jesting.

CLITANDER:
                    I am not.

CELIMENE:
                          Philinte plays *dress-up*?

PHILINTE:
No, I do *not*.

CLITANDER:
                    He wears a crown.

PHILINTE:
That is a lie—as is the sky-blue gown.

CELIMENE:
That specificity's a mite confusing.

PHILINTE:
A joke of Frank's—and *not* very amusing.

CELIMENE:
Don't be ashamed. I'll lend you my lamé.
But tell me, tell me, who'll we dish today?

ELIANTE:
Oh, Celimene, please don't. It's wicked. Cruel.

CELIMENE:
My cousin has a tender heart, the fool.
You see, I do impromptu portraits.

ELIANTE:
                                    Shameless.

CELIMENE:
All very innocent. The subjects nameless.

ELIANTE:
What of your litigants? Those whom you've stung
Who're suing you for your satiric tongue?

[*To* FRANK]

A court case, sir, which could be ominous.
Not all her targets stayed anonymous.

CELIMENE:
What I say in my home is my own doing.
Besides—those boneheads begged for barbecuing.

ELIANTE:
You go on trial tomorrow.

CELIMENE:

See this? Aloof.
And they can't win this case. They have no proof.
So who'll it be today? What fool, what pander?

CLITANDER:

I ran into Damis.

CELIMENE:

No names. No slander.

CLITANDER:

I met our friend named "D." . . . ?

CELIMENE:

Thank you, Clitander.
Take seats, take seats! More canapés, Dubois!

[DUBOIS *exits.* PHILINTE, ELIANTE, ACASTE, *and* CLITANDER *all seat them-
selves while* FRANK *remains conspicuously standing.*]

Monsieur? I guess a cushion's too bourgeois?

[FRANK *sits.*]

Good God. Congratulate me, kids. I've tamed him.

ACASTE:

Give us Damis! I'm sorry, have I named him?

[DUBOIS *enters with more canapés on his tray.*]

More food!

CELIMENE:

Yes, fodder for the outer rank.
Be sure to offer some to Father Frank.

And now, my friends, here is today's distraction:
"Portrait of D."

ELIANTE:

        I can't watch.

CLITANDER:

                Ready? Action!

CELIMENE:
"My name is D., yo, I'm so friggin' cool.
Sorry I'm wet. I just came from the pool.
Yeah, daily rounds. The six hours of Pilates.
The jog. The weights. Picked up a coupla hotties.
Chicks like my build. The way my shoulders pop.
I'm like a wedge with just a pea on top.
You know that I'm a lawyer. Yeah, it ain't so hard.
You wanna get divorced, babe? Here's my card."

CLITANDER:
It's Dam . . . It's *he*, down to that sleazy winking!

[*All applaud except* FRANK. DUBOIS *stands near* FRANK *offering him an hors d'oeuvre during the following.*]

FRANK:
Would you do this for "D." Be as unshrinking?
Or should I say, would you be as *unthinking*?

CLITANDER:
Don't look at me. I'm only in the chorus.

FRANK:
You raised this *cher amis,* Monsieur Clitoris.

CLITANDER:
Clitander.

FRANK:
>Whom I'm sure you'd rush to meet
And gush to, if you met "D." in the street.
You'd put Racine and all his ilk to shame
Especially if *Damis* (I'll say his name),
Damis, whose every fault was just now flaunted,
If this *dummy* had something that you wanted.
You'd frisk him for it like a practiced sleuth
And get it if you had to pull a tooth.

DUBOIS:
A canapé?

FRANK:
>No, thank you. GIVE ME *TRUTH*!

[FRANK *upends the salver, sending hors d'oeuvres flying.*]

Don't lie! Don't hug him! Don't soft-sell him so!
A man's a laughingstock? Then tell him so!

CELIMENE:
You are a laughingstock.

FRANK:
>This is a *person*.
What if he has some secret, private curse
On him? What if, at night, his cheeks are ashen?
So what's he won? Our laughter—or compassion?

CELIMENE:
Well, now we're really having fun. Dubois—
More canapés. Let's hear it for François!

[*Applause.* DUBOIS *exits.*]

Who's next, who's next?

ACASTE:

The Baroness Bélize!

I'm sorry, did I say it?

CELIMENE:

Quiet, please.

CLITANDER AND ACASTE:

Action!

CELIMENE [*idly twirling a lock of her hair*]:
"*My name's, like, B.? My skull's like full of air?*
Maybe it comes from twirling my, like, hair?
I've been like everywhere. Rome. Gstaad. Cadiz.
Where is that? God, I don't know where it is.
I just like went, like with my boyfriend Carlo?
We're great because our tastes like really are *low?*
Plus he's like, all, and I'm like, like, like like,
Like like like like, *like* like, *like like like . . .* like!"

[*Applause.* DUBOIS *enters with more canapés.*]

FRANK:
But why . . .

CELIMENE:

Yes, Frank?

FRANK:

Why *mix* with such buffoons?
And then why dare reduce them to cartoons?

ACASTE:
Don't look at me. Complain to Celimene.

FRANK:
It's you, you parasitic specimens
Of men who with your incense and your oil

Set her satiric spirit on the boil.
You've turned this woman to your trained coyote.
What might she be without you brain-free toadies?
A princess royal, were she not forced to sham.

CELIMENE:
I swear, monsieur, you see me as I am.

FRANK:
When I need your remarks, I'll ask, madame.
Mock fools for fun? Disparage such sad creatures?

CELIMENE:
Have you looked lately at your own sad features?

FRANK:
Do me behind my back. Play me on tour.
You be the hypocrite. I'm just a boor.

ACASTE AND CLITANDER:
Action!

CELIMENE:
"My name is F. (for Frank). Sweet Christ, I'm livid!
That's how I keep life interesting and vivid—
By scorning it. Good morning, sir, and damn you.
I hate you. Why? Perhaps because I am you.
You'll never speak, what with my blue-faced rages.
This modern world . . .

[*She bangs* DUBOIS's *tray.* DUBOIS *exits.*]

                      Give me the MIDDLE AGES!
When men were men and women could be had.
My eyes are rolling. Am I going mad?
Unhand me, sir! I'll stay and I'll survive.
Watch out. Protect your children. I'M ALIIIIIIIVE!"

[Huge applause, from FRANK, *too, the last one left applauding.]*

FRANK:
Bravo. Brilliant. But I don't leave that easily.

CELIMENE:
Damn.

FRANK:
      Tell me this: you've never queasily
Inquired how such performances might shock
Some of the sadly suffering folks you mock?
Do your late husband. Please—slice us a sample.

CELIMENE:
No one could play him. He was unexampled.
Unlike some.

PHILINTE:
           Frank, why pity all these fools
You'd mock yourself with even crueler tools?

CELIMENE:
Because his attitude's a fraud, a fiction.
He's only interested in contradiction.

ELIANTE:
I'll tell you why. Because Frank looks above.
He sees to the essential, which is *Love.*
He spots our faults and knows we must be better.
He peers beyond our foolishness, the fetters
Of ignorance and lies and lust and greed
That keep us from those goods we truly need.
He's like a doctor fighting an infection
Or like a lover sighting love's perfection.
That's why he rants and rails and plays the scourge:
He's summoning the perfect to emerge.

See with my eyes, he says, cast off myopia,
And share with me my vision of utopia,
For heaven hangs just here above our heads!
Reach up, he cries! Hate lies! Love Man instead!

FRANK:
I didn't understand a thing you said.
Love *Man*? A race fit only for destruction?

ELIANTE:
Your rage displays the strength of your seduction.

[BASQUE *enters and stands at the edge of the room. He is a lumpish, ill-dressed servant, played by the same actor who plays* DUBOIS.]

BASQUE:
Monsieur . . .

FRANK:
                A pox on humankind, I say!

ELIANTE:
Your anger's an affectionate display.

BASQUE:
Monsieur . . .

ELIANTE:
                I know you're needy, Frank. You're human.

FRANK:
I'm nothing of the kind. Stop *simpering,* woman!

ELIANTE:
You're damaged. Vulnerable. So drop the act.

FRANK:
How dare you say I'm vulnerable? Stay back!

BASQUE:
Monsieur . . .

CLITANDER:
        Good God, what's that? Call the police.

FRANK:
That's my valet.

CLITANDER:
          This clot of rancid grease?

BASQUE:
That's me.

CLITANDER:
       You stink.

BASQUE:
           It's part of my renown.
So, hey. Are you the drag queen with the crown?

PHILINTE:
There is no crown!

BASQUE:
         Oh, so it's you? Well, no surprise.

[*To* FRANK]

Monsieur, a man came for you. About this size.
He had a penis.

FRANK:
      What?

[BASQUE *produces a paper.*]

BASQUE:
                                    To come to court.
Something about a poem, and a wart . . .

FRANK:
Not now.

BASQUE:
                    He said . . .

FRANK:
                                    Not now.

BASQUE:
                                            You can't postpone this.
He wore this fancy coat.

CLITANDER:
                                    Sir, if you own this,
Take it away.

FRANK:
                        I'm sorry he's distressed you.

BASQUE:
He said . . .

FRANK:
            NOT NOW!

BASQUE:
                            He said they would arrest you.

FRANK:
You see this frown?

BASQUE [*indicating* PHILINTE]:
                            Her Majesty's a witness.

PHILINTE:
There is no gown!

[FRANK *and* BASQUE *huddle.* CELIMENE *pulls* PHILINTE *aside.*]

CELIMENE:
Philinte, what is this business?

PHILINTE:
A dustup with Oronte and Frank.

CELIMENE:
Oronte . . . ?

PHILINTE:
He read, and Frank called him a dilettante.

CELIMENE:
He what?

PHILINTE:
Frank doesn't pride himself on shyness.
So I'm apparently . . .

BASQUE [*as he exits, to* PHILINTE]:
(*YOO-HOO!*)

PHILINTE:
. . . Her Royal Highness.

CELIMENE:
I need Oronte to testify in court.
I could be ruined without Oronte's support.
Will you please beg your pal for palliation?

[EVERYONE *freezes except* PHILINTE.]

PHILINTE [*aside, to audience*]:
But here's my chance for sweet retaliation!
This fib about my bent for sky-blue drag . . .

[*To someone in the audience*]

(I saw that look. It was a lie. A *gag.*)
. . . I'll pay Frank back. I'll bend veracity.
I'll medicate him—with mendacity!

[ALL *unfreeze.*]

CELIMENE:
So will you help, or do I have to stab him?

PHILINTE:
No, wait. Wait. Celimene, you've got to grab him.
Do you know who Frank is?

CELIMENE:
                              A poltergeist?
Attila's ghost, perhaps? The Anti-Christ?

PHILINTE:
That kook there is *King Louis's bastard brother.*
François the Lost. With influence like none other.

CELIMENE:
This kook's a duke—?

PHILINTE:
                      With wealth to soothe all woes.

CELIMENE:
But what about the look, the low-rent clothes?

PHILINTE:
That's part of his disguise. It's all a pose.
Help needy damsels. That's His Grace's credo.

CELIMENE:
You mean he's here to help me . . . ?

CELIMENE AND PHILINTE:

> . . . *incognito*!

FRANK:

All right, so idiocy's won. Where's my hat?

CELIMENE:

Your Grace—but Frank, you can't leave just like that.

FRANK:

Oh, can't I?

CELIMENE:

> Well, I hope we'll get to see you.

FRANK:

Of that delight, madame, I'm glad to free you.

CELIMENE:

No, really. Do come back. Come back today.

FRANK:

For what? Act Two of your satiric play?

CELIMENE:

For me. I'd love to come to learn you better.
Without this riffraff we can speak unfettered.

[FRANK *pulls* PHILINTE *aside.*]

FRANK:

Philinte . . . What's turned this wolf into an Irish setter?
Batting her lashes, bathing me in drool . . .

PHILINTE:

You didn't guess? Why, she's in love, you fool.

FRANK:

Who with?

PHILINTE:

        With you! "I'd love to come to learn you"?
Love to? Good God, man, Celimene would *yearn* to!

FRANK:

But all her snips and sneers?

PHILINTE:

                A loving sham.
A cover for a heaving diaphragm.

FRANK:

Heaving with hate, perhaps. Or tightly knotted.
Love *me*?

PHILINTE:

      My friend, the woman is besotted.

FRANK:

I did note certain signs of amorous warning . . .

PHILINTE:

It's love.

FRANK:

      But how? We only met this morning!

PHILINTE:

Forget your dawdling Anglo-Saxon dance.
Love happens in an eyeblink here in France.

FRANK:

Then I shall love her, too! If just from pity.
Why not? She's charming, not unhandsome, witty.
At heart like me. So simple, so naive . . .

[ORONTE *enters.*]

ORONTE:
Oh, no. That beast must go, or I shall leave!

CELIMENE:
No, no. You both must stay or I'll be grieved.

ORONTE:
He greeted my new song to you with silence,
Then adjectives of coprologic violence!

FRANK:
I won't retract one word, monsieur. Unhand me!
Not one word, *though the King himself command me!*

PHILINTE [*aside to* CELIMENE]:
(You hear that?)

CELIMENE:
              Frank. Oronte. You boys behave.

ORONTE:
I'm suing you, sir. I've dug your legal grave.

FRANK:
Only in France could rights become invalid
Because some ass-wipe wrote a crappy ballad.

CELIMENE:
It's taste! All taste!

ORONTE:
              I'll see you on the rack.

FRANK:
All right. I'll go for now. But I'll be back!

[FRANK *kisses* CELIMENE's *hand and exits, taking his hat from* DUBOIS.]

DUBOIS:
Madame . . .

CELIMENE:
                What news in court, Oronte? Am I a goner?

ORONTE:
No movement yet. I've spoken with His Honor.

DUBOIS:
Madame . . .

ORONTE:
                How can you stand that lout, for heaven's sake?

CELIMENE:
Inside, he's a dear. Outwardly, opaque.

DUBOIS:
MADAME.

CELIMENE:
                Yes, what do you want, Dubois? Just *say.*

DUBOIS:
You have a guest, madame. Arsinoé.

CELIMENE:
Yes, come—no doubt—to preen and smirk and gloat.
Well, please send in the sanctimonious goat.

[DUBOIS *exits.*]

She's behind this whole slander case, I know it.
Like some sad flasher she just has to show it.
Well, Satan's here. Will you excuse me, men?

[CELIMENE *shepherds out* ORONTE, ACASTE, *and* CLITANDER.]

ELIANTE:

What in the world did you tell Frank just then?

PHILINTE:

That she's in love with him.

ELIANTE:

Who?

PHILINTE:

Celimene.

ELIANTE:

She WHAT?!

PHILINTE:

All right, I lied. I fibbed. No quibbling.
And *her* I told that he's His Highness's sibling.

ELIANTE:

You fool! You fucking clown!

PHILINTE:

Eliante!

ELIANTE:

You *twat*!
You'll push them in each other's arms!

PHILINTE:

So what?
The prospect might be fun.

ELIANTE:

You're so unfeeling.
Don't ever speak to me again!

PHILINTE:

I'm reeling!

ELIANTE:
You . . . *man*! I should have known you had no heart.
You bring this god and then force us to part?

PHILINTE:
What god?

ELIANTE:
       God *Frank.*

PHILINTE:
                   You're giving me the jimjams.

ELIANTE:
I'm going to tell my cousin of your flimflams
Then move to someplace suitably remote
And dote upon the oats, or rather, *oat*
I never sowed—all thanks to you, take note!

PHILINTE:
Eliante!

[ELIANTE *exits in tears.* PHILINTE *follows her as* DUBOIS *enters.*]

DUBOIS:
Arsinoé. The sanctimonious goat.

[DUBOIS *clears his throat and begins again.*]

Arsinoé.

[CELIMENE *reenters.*]

CELIMENE:
      A spider dipped in talcum . . .

[ARSINOÉ *enters.*]

ARSINOÉ:

Dear Celimene!

CELIMENE:

Arsinoé! (*Mwah.*) Welcome!
How *are* you? Where've you *been*? You've got a nerve!
You never write—Dubois, some more hors d'oeuvres.

[DUBOIS *exits.*]

ARSINOÉ:

I'm sorry to intrude on you sans warning.
I think you go on trial tomorrow morning . . . ?

CELIMENE:

On trial? Oh, that. I totally forgot!
Sans you, I would have. But you know it's not
As if there's proof to make these charges viable.
Sans written evidence there is no libel.
So shall we sit or would you rather go?
My door is always open, as you know.
Wiedersehen!

ARSINOÉ:

Celimene, I've come to aid you.

CELIMENE:

Aid me . . . ?

ARSINOÉ:

Against the gossip that has made you
The focus of so much malicious chat.
To tell you what vile filth is being spat
About you in salons around our city.
To show my friendship, my concern, my pity.
I was last night with certain goodly folk,
Fine Christians all, yet when of *you* they spoke—

Of course they praised your wit, your style, etcet'ra—
But what my brethren did not praise (and bet'ra
Millstone be tied to me, to cite our Savior)
They did not praise your, shall we say, *behavior.*
This constant crush of guests whom you attract,
So many men, for instance, may detract
(*They* felt) from your good name and reputation.
Of course I parried each insinuation,
But what could I alone, or how rebut
Such terms as *tart, whore, floozy, trollop, slut*—
All used of you? I'd never heard such smut!
And from their mouths, who're charity's own pattern!
Prostitute. Strumpet. Baggage. Hussy. Slattern.
(Don't think I'm gossiping. I'm not the sort.
I never gossip, dear. I just report.)
Fornicatrix! (The air was almost scarlet.)
Jade! Concubine! Kept woman! Poxy harlot!
In any case, such are the wicked slurs
Your busy social calendar incurs.
I told them you'd slept with no guest. Not *any.*
My dear, how could you, since there are so many?
And *lesbian?* Not a chance. But now, it seems,
You've a new protégé who simply steams
With socio-sexual impropriety—
One Frank, too rank for fine society.
A bull. A bonobo. A foul-mouthed brute
To whom God knows what Christians might impute.
For instance, *cunnilingus. Sodomy.*
One doesn't need a full lobotomy
To see erotic discipline is called for
Or *what in God's name are my friends appalled for?*
Are they all *mad,* to wish you in a cell
Or *ROASTING IN SOME TOASTING DISH IN HELL?!*
Well, I'd go on but let's let that suffice.

I know you're much too wise for my advice
To be begrudged. My call to arms unheeded.
I bring you facts. Now self-control is needed.
Oh, I know self-control is hard to win.
But we must love the sinner, hate the sin.

CELIMENE:
Dear friend, I don't know how I can begin
To thank you. For, believe me, far from grudging
Your helpful homily, I sit here judging
How I, this instant, can pay you in kind,
Can show how little—very little—I mind
Such tattle. That your friends (who each I'm sure
Thinks him a Christian) could see paramours
In blameless guests, impurity in parties,
The End of Days in my much-envied soirées—
Such moral cretins don't deserve our blame.
Yet oddly I experienced the same
Regarding *you* last week! For at a gathering
Of certain dignities, we started blathering
Upon the theme of what makes someone "*good.*"
Your name came up, of course. That's understood.
But was I shocked to hear you called a fraud!
Your pious attitude called a façade!
Your moral zeal they called dissimulation,
Your daily trips to church an affectation
To let you ogle those young monks you court.
(Don't think I'm gossiping. I just report.)
And what could I alone, how use my wit
Against such terms as *prude, prig, hypocrite,*
Or this one: *two-faced canting Pharisee?*
Rebuttal would have seemed like heresy
Against a group united in its view
That not a single breath you draw is true.
They all agreed it's tragic, in a way.

For (quote) though celibate Arsinoé
Excoriates lust and fights in Jesus' camp
She paints her face like some Egyptian tramp.
And never mind her spate of priest-confessors,
What *she* needs is a first-rate hairdresser!
(Unquote.) You guess my answer to all this.
I said your hair was sui generis,
It's always been like that. A sort of log.
Your cutter does *not* have a seeing-eye dog.
But they were adamant, these otherwise
Intelligent, discerning folks. Her lies,
(They said, referring to your whole existence)
Are like some joke. If she showed such persistence
Examining her own soul—meaning yours—
Instead of everyone from Louis Quatorze
On down, she might see less disparity
And learn the meaning of true charity,
Might see to her own ethical reproof
Better to be a tart than be Tartuffe,
That moral advice presumes, before one gives it,
That one is moral and actually lives it.
Well, I'd go on but let's let that suffice.
I know you're much too wise for my advice
To be begrudged, my call to arms unheeded.
Our friends are idiots? *Understanding's* needed.
I know forgiveness can be hard to win.
But we must love the sinner, hate the sin.

[DUBOIS *has entered with a tray.*]

Hors d'oeuvre?

ARSINOÉ:
A shame one cannot diagnose a canker
And not meet incredulity and rancor.

CELIMENE:
I *crave* such mutual self-examination!
How swiftly we might stem contamination
If we stripped naked and then turned a cheek.
Let's do this, you and I—say, once a week?

ARSINOÉ:
You think that you're so smart.

CELIMENE:
                              My tragic flaw.

ARSINOÉ:
Well, *I'm* not smart.

CELIMENE:
                              There oughta be a law.

ARSINOÉ:
It wasn't I who called you louche, or tarty.

CELIMENE:
No, you just heard that from some second party.

ARSINOÉ:
You mock my looks like some low harridan?

CELIMENE:
Our natures we can't change. Our hair, we can.

ARSINOÉ:
Madame, I don't know why you use me so.

CELIMENE:
Then ask yourself why you traduce me so
In every drawing room, den, and convent basement.
Just don't come here with sneering self-effacement
To make me suffer for your own chagrins
Or damn me for your uncommitted sins.
That you've no crush of guests is not my doing,

And if you think we *screw,* you're misconstruing.
Nor can I help it it's not you they're wooing.
You want to meet Frank? Fine. Pick up a pen.
Just don't invade my house to sniff out men.
It's not my job to scratch your oily itch.

ARSINOÉ:
You BITCH!

[CELIMENE *bangs the salver, hors d'oeuvres fly, and* DUBOIS *exits.*]

        You think that you can simply flout,
Right to my face, the men you have about?

CELIMENE:
That's "flaunt" not "flout."

ARSINOÉ:
               You think I even care
That men line up to pay your entry fare?
Well I know worthy women with no suitors,
Women who're poetry, not a pair of hooters.
Who know that lovers can be found, when sought—
If one's prepared to sell what's cheaply bought.

CELIMENE:
You realize you slander me.

ARSINOÉ:
             I'm grieved.

CELIMENE:
I ought to sue.

ARSINOÉ:
          You wouldn't be believed.
Enough, madame. I would have taken leave
Some time ago, but I await my carriage.

CELIMENE:
Await it all the time you need—like marriage.

[CELIMENE *exits.* ARSINOÉ—*all alone—has a fit.*]

ARSINOÉ:
Gaaak! Agga. Fffp. Nyukh. Grrgkh. A LOG?! *Tsak! Woof!*
SEEING-EYE DOG?! *Eeeuw. Whopp!* I'LL GIVE YOU PROOF!
Proof. Proof. Proof. Proof . . . Woof . . . Woof . . .

[*She tears open a drawer and finds papers.*]

[ARSINOÉ *sniffs the room like a dog. She spots the desk.*]

Desk . . . Desk . . . !

HA HA!

[*She finds more papers, which she stuffs in her bag. She laughs madly.*]

HA HA HA HA HA HA HA HA HA . . .

[*She hears voices offstage.*]

. . . HA!

[ARSINOÉ *exits.* ACASTE, ORONTE, *and* CLITANDER *enter.*]

ORONTE:
Marquis, I've never known a man so calm.
In good times or in bad you win the palm.
You bask in such serene tranquility.
Pray, what's the source of such solidity?

ACASTE:

I'll tell you in a word: stupidity.
Stupidity unparalleled in man.
When I look in my mirror, as I can
A hundred times a day, not being employed,
I'm always glad to see me. Overjoyed.
For here I am, completely undeserving
Yet blessed with wealth and plenty. It's unnerving.
I'm cursed with youth, descended from a line
Renowned for nothing but its thirst for wine,
My ancestors all mad—oh, sorry, *nervous*.
Each one, including me, unfit for service.
I've imbecility fixed in my genes
Yet boast the most extravagant of means.
So tell me, sir, with nothing that could rankle,
What jerk on this God's earth would not be tranquil?
For I have everything a man might crave
Yet must (and will) do nothing till I reach my grave.
Still, I have talents—like urbanity—
To balance out my bland inanity.
Good teeth (you see?), fine profile, mindless brawn,
At plays I'm expert when I'm meant to yawn
Or when to snigger, when to shout "Bravo!"
(I watch the audience. That's how I know.)
With ladies—well, I get my share of pie.
Unlimited liquidity is why.
I know their card games, I know not to trump them,
Know when to rumple them and when to dump them,
Know where to hire a prostitute for sport . . .
The knowledge of a gentleman, in short.
And that's why I'm the calmest man at . . .

ORONTE:

                                        Court?

ACASTE:

                                                    . . . court.

CLITANDER:
Stupidity . . .

ACASTE:
                    I highly recommend it.

CLITANDER:
But what of Celimene? You've apprehended
Somehow that she'd accept you as a beau?

ACASTE:
Oh, more than apprehended, sir. I *know*.
Indeed, I came here to propose today.

[ACASTE *opens a box with a necklace.*]

CLITANDER:
Well, so did I.

[CLITANDER *opens a bigger box with a necklace.*]

ORONTE:
                    And I.

[ORONTE *opens a small box with a necklace.*]

ACASTE:
                        Why didn't you say?
If we're all interested, what could be fitter
Than that this broad go to the highest bidder?

ORONTE:
This lady's picky. Has she given a hint?

ACASTE:
That she's attracted? Not the slightest glint.
Treats me like furniture. She's nice and all,
But once mistook me for a parasol.

CLITANDER:
You don't resent such treatment? You don't mind?

ACASTE:
When you're as self-involved as me, you're blind.
I'm such a fool I think I still could win.

CLITANDER:
Stupidity, you say?

ACASTE:
                As thick as sin.

ORONTE:
I'll tell you what. Let's us three make a deal.
We'll each propose. If any of us feels
He's got a shot at marital survival—
The others yield the battle to their rival.

ACASTE AND CLITANDER:
Done!

[FRANK *enters in a gaudy coat, carrying a single large flower.*]

FRANK:
        Gentlemen. My friends. You've seen the weather?
Clouds drenched in pale pastels like angel feathers.
The air so pure, so soft, so *French*. Now scram.
I have important business with madame.

CLITANDER:
You dare, monsieur?

FRANK:

With deep serenity.

And take the Creep and the Obscenity.

[CLITANDER, ORONTE, *and* ACASTE *exit.* CELIMENE *enters.*]

CELIMENE:

Thank God! You're back. You dashing fashion plate!
Come sit by me where you can fulminate.

FRANK:

Madam, against my judgment, taste, or penchant
I find myself in love with you.

CELIMENE:

How trenchant.

FRANK:

Granted, I've only yearned for you an hour.
It makes my stomach turn, but here's a flower.

CELIMENE:

How sweet.

FRANK:

Oh, God, so it has come to this!

Reduced to flowers, and compliments, and bliss!

CELIMENE:

But sir, why should you compromise? Don't worry.
If you're so moved, let fly! Unleash a slurry.
Unwind. Vituperate.

FRANK:

You think?

CELIMENE:

Oh, do.

Pay me no mind. *To your own self be true.*

Your native honesty would prove defective
If you refrained from venomous invective.

FRANK:
Yes! Why need lovers lie, and cloy, and smile?
Your eyes are crooked. I have churning bile.

CELIMENE:
Indeed. Your unexpected declaration
Has sparked my own subgastric gurgitation.

FRANK:
It must be love.

CELIMENE:
           No doubt. Or may import
Uneasiness about my case in court.

[CELIMENE *goes to the desk and takes out papers.*]

Just look. Writs, depositions pro and con,
Subpoenas . . . No. *No.*

FRANK:
           What?

CELIMENE:
             Oh, no. They're gone!

FRANK:
What's gone?

CELIMENE:
           Oh, nothing. (Just some damning prose . . .)
Where were we? Stomach turning . . . Your new clothes . . .

FRANK:
Of course, you'll have to dump your other beaus.

CELIMENE:
  I what?

FRANK:
    If this is love, it's love exclusive.

CELIMENE:
  How dare you!—I don't mean to be abusive . . .

FRANK:
  Who are these men to you? What are you—kept?

CELIMENE:
  Oh, sir, a woman needs to be adept
  Given our society's male apparatus,
  For we have men's attention but no status.
  We have to learn to flatter, wheedle, stroke
  (I love that color, by the way), to joke
  And flirt (some wine?) and dicker with venality.
  A woman's pose is men's reality.

FRANK:
  You know your gaze is like a hazel flame?

CELIMENE:
  You know I'm toast if I don't win this claim?

FRANK:
  God damn it, woman, we're in love! We're smit!
  Why sully us with paralegal writ?

CELIMENE:
  I thought you might possess some wisdom on it.

FRANK:
  Forget your case. I've written you a sonnet.

[FRANK *takes out a paper and clears his throat to read.*]

CELIMENE:
Stop. *Stop.* Please. No. That's for my treasure shelf.

FRANK:
Not read?

CELIMENE:
       I doubt I could contain myself.
And there's the noise, the glare, this blustery weather . . .

DUBOIS:
A canapé?

[FRANK *takes one.*]

FRANK:
      When should we sleep together?

[CELIMENE *upends the salver, sending hors d'oeuvres flying.*]

CELIMENE:
What?!

DUBOIS:
    Shit!

[DUBOIS *exits.*]

FRANK:
      Why not? Let's live life with a yen.
For isn't that what love is for? Well, then?
Let's have it all, the whole absurd megillah!
Kisses, and sighs . . . ! We'll rent a quaint old villa
In Tuscany but never see a thing
We're so besotted by ourselves. We'll sing
Odd snatches of old love songs. Pick bouquets

The live-long afternoon . . . I seek your gaze
Across a daisied field. We run to us
And down we swoon, each one at one with Us,
A single quivering spoon, erasing sexes.
We'll scribble love notes signed with strings of X's.
Stroll down the beach (we're on a beach now) hand-
In-hand, and while we tread the trickly sand
We'll run the gamut of the sickly-sappy,
But oh, my God, my God, will we be happy!
Calling each other darling, pumpkin, pet,
Mein Liebchen, mi amor (wait, I'm not done yet)
And then when on the street (we're back in Paris)
We'll kiss at intersections, unembarrassed
At blocking traffic all the way to Spain.
We'll smooch in bars and in the driving rain,
Clinch in Clichy and rock the Trocadero!
Outdo the view in Rio de Janeiro!
We'll be so focused, such a single lens,
So all-in-all, we'll alienate our friends—
Of course, I haven't any, but what matter?
For we shall float above their envious chatter.
Our love will levitate us over life!
That is, at least until we're man and wife.
So what? Till then we'll lick love's slippery mango
While locked in our own private, zipless tango!

[FRANK *bends her over in a tango hold.*]

CELIMENE:
What paradise.

FRANK:

         And how.

[ELIANTE *enters.*]

ELIANTE:

Celimene . . .

CELIMENE:

Not now.

[ELIANTE *exits.*]

FRANK:
Have ever two so various, been so right?

CELIMENE:
Yet how can I, in my precarious plight,
Give thought to love?

FRANK:

Your plight?

CELIMENE:

Well . . .

FRANK:

Answer me.

CELIMENE:
I mean, of course, my case in Chancery.

FRANK:
What, that again? How dull, how trite, banal . . .

CELIMENE:
There's an officious, very tight cabal
Who'd love to ruin me.

FRANK:

O, I should have known!
How shallow.

CELIMENE:
        You, sir, callow to the bone
Tell *me* how I should order my existence?
Why are you here? Well—yes, at my insistence.
Why are you staring at me in this way?

FRANK:
You are magnificent. The Queen of May.
Good God, madame, why didn't you just *say*?

CELIMENE:
Say what . . . ?

FRANK:
        You loved me.

CELIMENE:
            Well . . .

FRANK:
                    Just, *bang,* declare it?
So say it now. "I love you." I can't bear it.

CELIMENE:
Sir, these days women must be circumspect.

FRANK:
Damn circumspection!

CELIMENE:
            If you would direct
Your short attention span to me, I'll finish.
My unforthcomingness does not diminish
My feelings . . .

FRANK:
        You have to say it—at top speed!
Do you love me?

CELIMENE:

    Well . . .

FRANK:

     You love me?

CELIMENE:

          Sir, what *need*

For open declarations? Look at us.
A moralist would throw the book at us
For cuddling here alone. Such private favor,
Is that not proof of how I feel, and savor
Your company?

FRANK:

    Do you love me?

CELIMENE:

        "*Love*," you say,

As if it were a cure, not a cliché.
You, so unsentimentally incautious,
So ever-prompt to say what makes you nauseous,
Would fall for love, that mess of mawkish goo?

FRANK:

Well . . .

CELIMENE:

   You, to whom there is no talking-to,
A loud-mouthed bull amid love's fragile china,
A rabid crackpot, you, the cackling mynah,
You'd opt for love, itself insanity,
A further spur to your volcanity?

FRANK:

Well . . .

CELIMENE:

       You, who're dedicated to the truth,
Would buy a ticket to the circus booth
Of love, that age-old mirror-maze of lies?

FRANK:

Eliante was right. Love sees with sharper eyes.
For underneath your artificial mask
I spy the other you—a powder flask
Of love. A woman honest, passionate, tender,
Who greets with joy whatever life may send her.
Who'll pity goldfish in a shallow bowl.
Who's soft at heart as a profiterole.

CELIMENE:

You've plumbed me to the bottom of my soul.

FRANK:

I knew it!

CELIMENE:

       Could you let a person finish?

FRANK:

Sorry.

CELIMENE:

      But sir, your own persona's thinnish.
I sense beneath your supercilious crust,
Your atrabilious ravings and disgust,
A puppy dog.

FRANK:

       A spaniel.

CELIMENE:

         Spaniel. Fine.
Whose barking is, at heart, a valentine.

FRANK:
What love can see the loveless never notice!
I am those things you say!

CELIMENE:
                              Yet what an onus
For you—that silly accidents of birth
Keep you from being what you might be on earth.

FRANK:
Which is . . . ?

CELIMENE:
                    A King.

FRANK:
                              And you would be my consort.
You are that now!

CELIMENE:
                    And you would help unsort
My case.

FRANK:
          Stop fretting! On a day like this?
We're blue-foot boobies on the Bay of Bliss,
Skimming atop its shimmering effervescence!

CELIMENE:
You're crazed.

FRANK:
              With love.

CELIMENE:
                              No, I mean crazed in essence.
And how could you and I become a dyad,
Between my jewelry and your jeremiads?

It's not as if we're destined, though you rant.
I'm not Eliante, who's fated for Philinte.

FRANK:

Am I not what you want? Just say. I'll change!
You'd be amazed at my dramatic range.
Am I not French enough? I'll parlay-voo,
Smoke black tobacco, wear a beret, too,
I'll read the Paris Existential News.
I'll shrug and smirk (like this). I'll sip Chartreuse.
Anything. Just as long as you're content.
I want to be the man whom you'd invent,
Your all-in-all, your friend and your confessor,
Your desert island disk, your un-depressor.
Oh, Sally, ditch these hothouse lords and ladies.
I'm Orpheus, come to summon you from Hades!

CELIMENE:
He used to call me Sally . . .

FRANK:

Who?

CELIMENE:

Alceste.
Who two eternal years has been at rest.
Pardon me, sir.

[CELIMENE *wipes her eyes.*]

FRANK:

You loved your husband, then?

CELIMENE:
Who wouldn't have? He was the best of men.

FRANK:
Pledge me your heart, I promise I'll be he.

CELIMENE:
I lost my heart when he was lost at sea.
A man so wise. So noble. Passionate. Manly.
He would've cleaned this case up spic-and-spanly
Were he alive . . .

FRANK:
                    Oh, not that goddamn case!

CELIMENE:
He was a paradigm. A separate race.

FRANK:
So now you throw this husband in my face?

CELIMENE:
He was as lofty as you're close to median.
He wasn't some self-pitying tragedian.
If he were here to see what life's become
He wouldn't stand around and suck his thumb.
I am in mortal danger, sir. So aid me!

FRANK:
You're right. Yes, yes, it's right that you upbraid me.
And yet I can't do much, in honesty.

CELIMENE:
Your Grace—François—what empty modesty.
A word to certain powers on high? Or higher . . . ?
A relative at court . . . ?

FRANK:
                    I've no one.

CELIMENE:
                              Liar.

FRANK:
Coquette.

CELIMENE:
     Lout.

FRANK:
          Leech.

CELIMENE:
               Wet blanket!

FRANK:
                    Hedonist!

CELIMENE:
                         Critic!

FRANK:
Isn't love wonderful? It's catalytic!
We two, who should be clawing at our throats,
Are lovebirds singing oriental notes!

[FRANK *sings a few of them, as* ORONTE *enters.*]

ORONTE:
Madame. *Madame.*

FRANK:
          Begone, you scrotum. Vanish!

ORONTE:
I have a question, and I'll not be banished,
Nor will I ask it with that person near.

CELIMENE:
I want you two to reconcile. You hear?
(For my sake? Frankie? Please?)

ORONTE:

                  I will if he will.

FRANK:

So be it. I forgive you for the evil
You've done me. I accept it with a shrug.
Now may I . . . Would you . . . Can I have a hug?

[FRANK *hugs* ORONTE. ORONTE *breaks away.*]

ORONTE:

It's *I* who's owed the damned apology!

FRANK:

Monsieur, I'll praise your every quality.
Your dancing skills, your sport, your *savoir veev'*,
The splendor of that wart, your snotted sleeve,
Your horsemanship, your cocksmanship, what have you.
But poetry? Um—*no*. I will not salve you
With compliments so richly undeserved.
I know that hurts. I know that you're unnerved.
My friend, I share your grief, your pain. Be gallant.
I'd be grieved, too, if I possessed your talent.

CELIMENE:

Well, there. Oronte, you see Frank's penitence . . .

ORONTE:

Madame, if you allow such denizens
Into your house then cross me off your list.
And you—expect some handcuffs on your wrist!
I'm not your butt!

FRANK:

               There is a faint suggestion . . .

[ORONTE *starts out, comes back.*]

ORONTE:

I never even got to ask my question!

FRANK:

If you mean "marry her," the answer's no.
Here comes your friend to ask it.

ORONTE:

                                        Madam . . .

FRANK:

                                                            Blow.

[ORONTE *exits.* CLITANDER *enters.*]

CLITANDER:

If I might have a word—in *private,* please.

FRANK:

I'm her advisor, her éminence grise.
Her fool, her fibrillator, and her florist.
But please, continue.

CLITANDER:

                        Well . . .

FRANK:

                                        Monsieur Clitoris.

CLITANDER:

Tander—Madame, your case comes up tomorrow,
To which I have contributed both borrowed
Moneys (I've lent you 20,000 francs
For which I've gotten nothing but your thanks),
Plus legal counsel, lawyers to you pro bono—

FRANK:

"Now will you marry me." How sweet! No, no,
Go on, please do.

CLITANDER:

                There's more I can attempt.
A gift to all the judges may preempt
Their verdict.

FRANK:

            Give them bribes is what you're saying.

CLITANDER:

I can support you. That's what I'm conveying,
And so will do, just let me marry you.

FRANK:

What, you—you *flea*?

CLITANDER:

              I wasn't asking you!

FRANK:

Woo her, woo me. You have to have us both.
We will not marry you! On that—our oath!

CLITANDER:

You parvenu! You meddling Jesuit!

CELIMENE:

Now really, sir! This man, so exquisite,
So princely, generous, brilliant, comme il faut,
For whom my house's doorways are too low,
You treat like some plebeian, boorish peasant?

CLITANDER:

I had hoped this occasion would be pleasant.
I'll come back in an hour.

FRANK:

             You void! You figment!

[CLITANDER *exits.*]

FRANK:
Alone at last. Thank God we're rid of *them*.

CELIMENE:
But don't you want to plan your stratagem?

[FRANK *strokes her arm.*]

FRANK:
My stratagem . . .

CELIMENE:
                              Or even (stop that) effect it?

FRANK:
Your case?

CELIMENE:
              My case.

FRANK:
                              But, pumpkin, you're protected.

CELIMENE:
By you.

FRANK:
              By love!

CELIMENE:
                              And you. And royal "friends."

FRANK:
That regal providence that shapes our ends.
High Cupid backs our side. Let that propel you!

[*They kiss, passionately.*]

ELIANTE [*from offstage*]:
Celimene!

[*The two break away breathless as* ELIANTE *enters.*]

I have something I must tell you.

CELIMENE:
Oh, not now, El, my platter's rather full.

ELIANTE:
Frank doesn't love you and he has no pull!
He's no relation to the royal household!

[CELIMENE *doesn't hear a word of it, nor does* FRANK.]

CELIMENE:
Darling, let's talk when I'm not quite so tousled.

[*To* FRANK]

And you . . . You'll do that thing we talked about?

FRANK:
I'm desolate at this display of doubt.

ELIANTE:
It's all a LIE!

CELIMENE:
All right, well then . . . Bye-bye.

[CELIMENE *exits.*]

FRANK:
And they say love is blind.

ELIANTE:

I wouldn't know.

FRANK:

But this reminds me . . . Yes, before I go
There's something that I must tell *you.*

ELIANTE:

Indeed, sir?

Given all the lies about, why should I heed, sir?

FRANK:

You're loved.

ELIANTE:

I'm what?!

FRANK:

You're loved.

ELIANTE:

By whom?

FRANK:

A man.

Let him remain anonymous.

ELIANTE:

Some fan?

FRANK:

You are the sun in his Copernican
Universe. Minus you he's some lost planet
Adrift in empty space. Your eyes began it.

ELIANTE:

My face?

FRANK:
      Your eyes. He saw them and he fell.
He pines for you but is too shy to tell.

ELIANTE:
I know this man?

FRANK:
          He's in this house.

ELIANTE:
                    Who is he?

FRANK:
Your predetermined spouse.

ELIANTE:
             Monsieur, I'm dizzy!

FRANK:
He has his faults.

ELIANTE:
        Might he be . . . doctrinaire?

FRANK:
He might work up a lather.

ELIANTE:
           Debonair?

FRANK:
I wouldn't say that. Rather . . .

ELIANTE:
              Speaks with relish?

FRANK:
Yes, when he speaks.

ELIANTE:
But plainly?

FRANK:
Unembellished.

ELIANTE:
He's brilliant?

FRANK:
I suppose he's had a thought.

ELIANTE:
The model of the soul mate whom I've sought!
Oh God, I see that man before me now.

FRANK:
Where?

ELIANTE:
In my mind's eye. Yes, his noble brow.
Great flashing eyes. Well-built and very sexy.

FRANK:
Who, he?

ELIANTE:
Your tendency to apoplexy.

FRANK:
We're speaking of this other guy.

ELIANTE:
"I see."

FRANK:
Although God knows how love can change a man.
I swear today I don't know what I am.
Am I a cynic, snarky and morose?

Or Romeo, given a homeopathic dose?
And who could love, or find love's incandescence
In someone so confused about his essence?

ELIANTE:
You're much too meek. About *"this man,"* I mean.
He owned my love the moment he was seen.

FRANK:
You mean you actually can stand the dork?

ELIANTE:
This eagle come to earth as humble stork?
This blazing star to any other men?

FRANK:
That's a bit far.

ELIANTE:
               But what of Celimene?
"Those two" aren't locked in passionate collusion?

FRANK:
Listen, he's soft, not subject to delusion.
No, no, madame. It's your heart he salutes.

ELIANTE:
Oh, sir. I love him, too!

FRANK:
                    No.

ELIANTE:
                      Yes! His boot's
Too good for me to lick. I am not worthy!

FRANK:
What crap. You two are equal in the earthy
Department. You may be a porcelain clock

But you're a woman and he's got a cock,
So tell him!

ELIANTE:

Tell him . . . ?

FRANK:

Yes! He's not above you!

ELIANTE:

Tell him?

FRANK:

Give him the works!

[ELIANTE *throws herself on him.*]

ELIANTE:

Oh, Frank, I love you!

FRANK:

You *WHAT*?!

[ELIANTE *pursues him around the room.*]

ELIANTE:

I know I'm sweet, I'm saccharine,
But I can change! I'll change from porcelain
To tempered iron, from sugarcane to rum,
I'll be a tiger! You're fantastic! Come,
Let's run away! We needn't even marry!
Take my virginity! Why have I carried
It all these years but for a mate like you!
Have me right here! Let's copulate! Let's screw!
Order me, Frank! Command me and I'll follow.
You're right, this world's a sty! Let's wallow! Wallow!
Take me, Frank! Do it to me while I'm dizzy!

[*By now she's got him on the floor, and straddles him.* PHILINTE *has entered during this.*]

PHILINTE:
Eliante!

ELIANTE:
　　　Oh, Jesus, can't you see I'm *busy*?
Don't stop us. Damn the man who interferes!
I'll stab you through the heart with pinking shears!

PHILINTE:
I don't believe this! Frank, this can't be true!

FRANK:
It is!

ELIANTE [*to* FRANK]:
　　　If we don't copulate, I'll kill you, too.
The choice is yours, you stud: die, or deflower.
I'll come back for your answer in an hour.

[ELIANTE *kisses* FRANK *passionately.*]

That little kiss can set your timer going.

[*To* PHILINTE]

And as for you—your panty-line is showing.

[ELIANTE *exits.*]

PHILINTE:
Eliante! Eliante, wait! Please, don't go away!

FRANK:
They love me!

PHILINTE:

It can't be . . . !

[DUBOIS *enters with a tray.*]

DUBOIS:

A *canapé* . . . ?

[DUBOIS *bangs the tray himself, sending hors d'oeuvres flying.*]

[*CURTAIN.*]

ACT 2

[*The same, picking up where we left off with* FRANK, PHILINTE, *and* DUBOIS.]

DUBOIS:

A *canapé* . . . ?

[DUBOIS *bangs his tray, sending hors d'oeuvres flying, and exits.*]

PHILINTE:
They love you?

FRANK:

Not just one, but both of them!
Red-hot Eliante and sassy Celimene.

PHILINTE:
Listen . . .

FRANK:

"*Your Grace,*" she calls me. God knows why.

PHILINTE:
It's my fault, Frank.

FRANK:
                No, no. *François.*

PHILINTE:
                                I *lied.*
I lied to you. *I made this up.* You hear?

FRANK:
You're absolutely right. Celimene's more dear.

PHILINTE:
But—

FRANK:
        Yes. Good point. Eliante's your type. You have her.

PHILINTE:
Not after what I heard of your palaver.
Let's screw, she says? The sweet, the chaste Eliante?

FRANK:
Beneath that chastity, she's a bacchante.

PHILINTE:
You dog! You shit!

FRANK:
               I tried to plead your suit.
She jumped on me and offered me her loot.

PHILINTE:
So much for all your principles, you traitor!

FRANK:
But look, when this blows over you can date her.

PHILINTE:
And Celimene? With *you,* the Scourge of God?

FRANK:
Amazing. And you know what's really odd?
We share the same opinions, same ideas . . .

PHILINTE:
François, she's Cleopatra. She's *Medea*.

FRANK:
I can't explain it. She exalts my soul.
She's single malt. She's rain. She's rock-and-roll.

PHILINTE:
She doesn't care you have no gold or trinkets?

FRANK:
I couldn't love her if I didn't think it.

PHILINTE:
She *makes* you think it. She's a prize coquette!

FRANK:
Yet just an hour ago, pray don't forget,
She was your shining social luminary.

PHILINTE:
And will you time-share with Tom, Dick, and Harry?

FRANK:
Those clowns? They're nothing. She's as good as said.
And if they're not, I'll shoot the bastards dead.

PHILINTE:
So what's your secret, in all modesty?

FRANK:
For sex? Just be yourself! Use *honesty*.
I swear, express whatever's on your mind.
Before you know it, you'll be intertwined
And on the carpet like Eliante and me,
About to blend.

PHILINTE:

                Thanks for reminding me.

FRANK:

With truthful words, my friend, we breathe our heart.
A woman wants your matter, not your art.
Let's try it. I'll impersonate your lady.
And you be you, but truthful. Nothing weighty,
Whatever comes to you. Just let it out.

PHILINTE:

Hello, Eliante. How're you?

FRANK:

                    Don't mumble. *Shout*!

PHILINTE:

HELLO, ELIANTE !

FRANK:

               Much better. Give me *vigor.*

PHILINTE:

YOU'RE LOOKING WELL!

FRANK:

                    I'm not.

PHILINTE:

                    You're not?

FRANK:

                           Rigor,

Philinte. What if I *don't* look well? Proceed.

PHILINTE:

YOU CERTAINLY DO LOOK LIKE HELL!

FRANK:

No need
To deafen me. Go on.

PHILINTE:

How?

FRANK:

Give me details.

PHILINTE:
You're looking . . . bigger.

FRANK:

Good.

PHILINTE:

You'll be a she-whale
If you keep eating sweets—She really will.

FRANK:
So tell her!

PHILINTE:

Stop ingesting sugary swill!
Give up the Junior Mints!

FRANK:

Nice and specific.

PHILINTE:
I will not wed a human blintz!

FRANK:

Terrific.
Now that you've softened her with candor—*pounce.*

[BASQUE *enters and observes all this.*]

PHILINTE:

I love you.

FRANK:

    Me?

PHILINTE:

        Yes, you. Just lose an ounce.

BASQUE:

Monsieur . . .

FRANK:

       You love me how, pray tell?

PHILINTE:

               So needily.

FRANK:

You don't!

PHILINTE:

    I do! If you could know how greedily
I dream of you . . .

FRANK:

       Specifics.

PHILINTE:

           . . . and your breasts.

FRANK:

My breasts?

PHILINTE:

     I mean your TITS!

[CELIMENE *and* ELIANTE *enter, unnoticed by* FRANK *and* PHILINTE.]

FRANK:

My, my!

PHILINTE:

Lip-rests
For Jupiter which in my dreams I suckle,
Until both knees and lungs begin to buckle.

BASQUE:

Monsieur . . .

FRANK:

Come on, what else?

PHILINTE:

Your mouth.

FRANK:

Don't truckle.

PHILINTE:

Your thighs which, even though I've never seen them,
Yet in my dreams . . .

FRANK:

Say it!

PHILINTE:

. . . I slide between them!

FRANK:

Yes! Good!

PHILINTE:

I cup your buttocks for support.

FRANK:

Fantastic.

BASQUE:
> You're both wanted, down at court.

FRANK:
Not now!

PHILINTE:
> *Your cheeks are fleshy, satin, gorgeous . . .*

FRANK:
Where are we doing this?

PHILINTE:
> My club. The St. George's.
The leather sofa on the second floor,
While someone watches, peeping at the door.
That witness somehow opens all our sluices,
That sets our blood astir, makes flow our juices,
I do what *you* want, then *you* do what *I* want,
And then I see our peeping Tom's . . . *Eliante!*

CELIMENE:
What did cook put in those hors d'oeuvres, I wonder.

PHILINTE:
Eliante, I love you. *Need* you. Let me thunder
It, *I ADORE YOU!* Dream of you! I cup
Your buttocks nightly! Sometimes more! I sup
At the taut udders of your aureoles . . .

[*Losing steam*]

I suck your . . . candied lips, those . . . gloryholes . . .
To heaven . . .

[ELIANTE *hasn't heard a word.*]

ELIANTE:
What?

PHILINTE:
For it was you I spoke to.
It wasn't Frank I dreamt I gave a poke to.
Frank was a stand-in, here to lend support!

ELIANTE:
Hello, Frank.

FRANK:
Actually, we're off to court.
That bit of business needs to be attended—?

CELIMENE:
You let me know when fences have been mended.

FRANK:
Fear not, madame. My influence is royal.
Reason shall wear the crown on France's soil!

[FRANK *exits.*]

PHILINTE:
Those gloryholes were improv. Blame my youth.
As for your buttocks—that is God's own truth!

[PHILINTE *exits.*]

ELIANTE:
I've a confession, cuz.

CELIMENE:
I, too, have tidings.

ELIANTE:
You first.

CELIMENE:
      No, you.

ELIANTE:
          No, you.

CELIMENE:
              There's no use hiding . . .

ELIANTE:
All right, I'll tell you. I'm in love!

CELIMENE:
                Hurray!

ELIANTE:
It's quite a whirlwind, happening in one day . . .

CELIMENE:
Come on! I knew you two would get together!

ELIANTE:
You knew?

CELIMENE:
        Oh, please! The only question's whether
I augured this the minute you two met!
Was he not here just now, a live gazette
For how he feels, love blazing from his pupils?
You're tethered at the hip, you two. Your scruples,
Your seriousness . . . You're joined by gravity.

ELIANTE:
We almost copulated. *Avidly.*

CELIMENE:
Somewhat untypical.

ELIANTE:

           Right on this rug.

CELIMENE:

Apocalyptical.

ELIANTE:

       He's like some drug.
I grant he's rather cool.

CELIMENE:

        He's that.

ELIANTE:

                But stoic.
Out of some other age. Noble. Heroic.

CELIMENE:

You're kidding me.

ELIANTE:

       He's Hamlet. He's Le Cid.
And underneath it all—a raging id.

CELIMENE:

Yet just now you were undemonstrative.

ELIANTE:

For fear that you would get remonstrative.
Oh, I'm so glad you didn't buy that hoax!

CELIMENE:

That what?

ELIANTE:

     Philinte. Who has no gift for jokes,
Being such a pillar of veracity.
Why would he stoop to such mendacity?
Frank is King Louis's brother!

CELIMENE:

So you *know*?

ELIANTE:

And all the rest of it. Well, ho, ho, ho!

CELIMENE:

I've no idea what that means, but basta!
And here's another something for the roster:
I'm in love, too.

ELIANTE:

Hooray!

CELIMENE:

And as you say,
It's rather overwhelming, in one day.

ELIANTE:

We'll have a double wedding, Celimene!

CELIMENE:

I never thought that I could love again
After Alceste. I felt at best unfitted.
And now I love, it's so hard to admit it.
What were more unforeseen, what could be grander?

ELIANTE:

So which one won? Oronte, Acaste, Clitander?

[DUBOIS *enters.*]

DUBOIS:

Madame . . .

CELIMENE:

Oronte, Acaste . . .

DUBOIS:

Madame . . .

CELIMENE:

Clitander?

Why're we discussing *them*?

ELIANTE:

Aren't they germane?

For one of them's your love.

CELIMENE:

Are you insane?

DUBOIS:

Madame . . .

ELIANTE:

Who is it, then?

CELIMENE:

Well, Frank, of course.

ELIANTE:

Frank?!

CELIMENE:

Frank.

ELIANTE:

You know for certain? What's your source?

CELIMENE:

I am!

DUBOIS:

MADAME.

CELIMENE:

And *he* is! He confessed it!

ELIANTE:
And you just swallowed that? Unpredigested?

CELIMENE:
I know it's weird. I know that it's a switch.

ELIANTE:
(Oh, no! I'll kill the lying sonofabitch . . .)

CELIMENE:
I can't explain it. He exalts my soul.

ELIANTE:
But Celimene, the man assaults your whole . . .

CELIMENE:
Existence. Yes, the whole thing's risible.

DUBOIS:
Yo! HEY! What am I, invisible?

ELIANTE:
Well, who am *I* in love with, then?

CELIMENE:
                    Philinte!

[PHILINTE *enters, unnoticed, carrying a single flower.*]

ELIANTE:
Philinte? What, that transvestite spinster aunt?

[PHILINTE *quickly exits, still unnoticed.*]

CELIMENE:
It seems a natural . . .

ELIANTE:
                    That German spinet?

DUBOIS:
May I have your attention for a minute,
Amidst your pressing intimate affairs?

CELIMENE:
What is it, please?

DUBOIS:
                    Arsinoé's downstairs.

CELIMENE:
That snake! She stole some letters from my desk,
Now she returns in triumph. It's grotesque . . .

ELIANTE:
So you and Frank . . .

CELIMENE:
                    The woman has no honor.

ELIANTE:
So you and Frank . . .

CELIMENE:
                    I know! I'll sic Frank on her!
He'll cut her down to size and never swerve!
But wait a moment . . . Where are the hors d'oeuvres?

DUBOIS:
I'm sorry, did I fall behind the curve?
Hors d'oeuvres you want? Hell, lemme check the kitchen.
Some canapés? Why not? Your guests can pitch 'em
Into my *fricking face* all night and day!
I'll serve *hors d'oeuvres*. Now where's my little tray?

[DUBOIS *exits.*]

CELIMENE:
He seems distraught.

ELIANTE:

             All right, then have it *your* way!
You take him! Fine! I'll make the sacrifice.
I've had a lot of practice being *nice*.

CELIMENE:
But darling—

ELIANTE:

          You're in love! Elate! Transformed!
I guess that *I* was sadly *misinformed*!

[ELIANTE *exits in tears.*]

CELIMENE:
There's something *off* today. Some point I'm missing . . .

[ARSINOÉ *enters.*]

ARSINOÉ:
Dear Celimene!

CELIMENE:

          Let's do without the kissing.
Or let me don a sturdy turtleneck
To obviate two pinholes from your peck.

[DUBOIS *enters with a tray of hors d'oeuvres, flinging them gaily by handfuls into the air.*]

DUBOIS:
Canapés! Canapés!

[DUBOIS *sloppily stuffs his mouth with canapés.*]

         Mmmmm! A canapé?

CELIMENE:
Thank you, Dubois. I see you found your tray.

[DUBOIS *frisbees the tray into the room and exits.*]

CELIMENE:
Already back to steal more personal papers?
What do the Gospels say about such capers?

ARSINOÉ:
The Gospels tell us blessed are the meek.
And meek you'll be—*in jail*—this time next week.
After your letters raise the judge's hackles
He'll fetter you up to the neck in shackles.

CELIMENE:
I doubt it. I've a patron. I'm immune.

ARSINOÉ:
You always liked to sing a cocky tune,
Yet were more coy. Not such an overreacher.

CELIMENE:
I've been instructed by an expert teacher.

[FRANK *enters.*]

Speak of the devil. Arsinoé—Frank.
I'll let him slay you with his party pranks.
So, pumpkin, you just be yourself, ha ha.
(What news at court?)

FRANK:
                    (I'm hard at work.)

CELIMENE:
                              Ta-ta!

[CELIMENE *exits.*]

ARSINOÉ:
So you're the mystery man. Your fame precedes you.
Welcome to Sodom, sir. Our country needs you.
Oh, come, come, come, come, *come.* No humble words.
France needs a male who doesn't run in herds
Or laze in fields just grazing the alfalfa.
We need a superman, a stud, an alpha
Who doesn't truckle, pander, or defer.
So which position, sir, would you prefer?

FRANK:
Position . . . ?

ARSINOÉ:
              Servicing the state. What portal
Wouldn't gape for such a more-than-human mortal?

FRANK:
But I . . .

ARSINOÉ:
              See that? A modest man, but quick,
Whose merits blend the carrot *and* the stick.
A man, I say? A Zeus to halt this crisis.
A savior, a hero, a Dionysus.
A rod of iron! A gushing font! A force!
What ecstasy to have this intercourse.
We only met—see how you've penetrated?
Two minutes' talk, and lo! behold me sated.

FRANK:
You're kind—

ARSINOÉ:
              Arsinoé. No, *you* are kind.
But then at Celimene's I always find

Company that shines, that glitters, that transcends
The mere banal.

FRANK:

        So Celimene's a friend?

ARSINOÉ:

My oldest, dearest, closest pal. The End.
But tell me of your plans, your high ambitions.

FRANK:

I have none, given my Doric disposition.

ARSINOÉ:

But that's where you come in. A man so moral
Is made to wear this country's highest laurel.

FRANK:

I?

ARSINOÉ:

  You.

FRANK:

      I've won no war, done no great deed.

ARSINOÉ:

For such as you, fine sir, there is no need.
Would you leave France to chattering parvenus?

FRANK:

But say I wanted . . . France . . . what avenues
Are open but corruption's rotten fen?

ARSINOÉ:

But that's where you come in. You cleanse this den
And flourish!

FRANK:

     These days idiots are acclaimed.

ARSINOÉ:

And that's where you come in. Could you be blamed
For flying truth's flag, reforming lying manners?

FRANK:

But every moron's out there flying banners.

ARSINOÉ:

And that's where you come in. This is the hour
To claim your natural birthright.

FRANK:

                              Which is—?

ARSINOÉ:

                                             Power.

FRANK:

Power . . . !

ARSINOÉ:
          Fame.

FRANK:

                    Fame . . . !

ARSINOÉ:

                              France's rings are closed, concentric.
You're something we are not.

FRANK:

                    Eccentr—?

ARSINOÉ:

                              Authentic.
And like some subterranean ooze or sap
You'll rise until you flow from every tap.
Nor would you let your high position blind you.

FRANK:
Never.

ARSINOÉ:
      Not with the right woman behind you.

FRANK:
And that's where you . . . ?

ARSINOÉ:
                       And that's where I come in.

FRANK:
I *have* that woman, though. It's Celimin. *Men.*

ARSINOÉ:
Yes, well . . .

FRANK:
           I have one question, though, that's burning.
How did she never mention so discerning
And so intelligent a friend as you?

ARSINOÉ:
She's otherwise engaged these days.

FRANK:
                     It's true.
This hideous court case certainly must hover.

ARSINOÉ:
To tell the truth, I meant her secret lover.

FRANK:
Her what . . . ?

ARSINOÉ:
          This new one, now she's had each lad,
Groom, butler, baron, clergyman, and cad
In town. You didn't know that?

FRANK:

No.

ARSINOÉ:

My bad.
Men seem to stick to her magnetically.

FRANK:
But how . . . ?

ARSINOÉ:

She picks them alphabetically.
Why, Celimene's a whore so loose she's leaking.

FRANK:
This is your dearest friend of whom you're speaking?

ARSINOÉ:
And I *adore* the girl, cellar to roof.

FRANK:
She has a lover . . . ?

ARSINOÉ:

Yes. And I have proof.

BASQUE [*from offstage*]:
Monsieur . . . !

ARSINOÉ:

Crush notes to her inamorato
That prove her purity's a weekly lotto.

FRANK:
She doesn't love me, then?

ARSINOÉ:

You—and a myriad.

FRANK:
Well, then, she doesn't love me, period.

ARSINOÉ:
Escort me home for further confirmation
And what I might provide as . . . consolation . . .

[ARSINOÉ *exits as* BASQUE *enters, dressed for traveling, with a suitcase in either hand and bent beneath the weight of a huge trunk strapped to his back.*]

FRANK:
Perfidious woman! Making me her slave . . .

BASQUE:
Monsieur!

FRANK:
     The bitch!

BASQUE:
               If you can hear me, wave.

FRANK:
I sensed as much. That's why my heart misgave.

BASQUE:
Hey! Don Giovanni! Time to go, you dig?

FRANK:
What is all this? What's this ridiculous rig?

BASQUE:
The jig is up, monsieur. Check out the note.

FRANK:
What note?

BASQUE:
          I know it's here. I put it in my coat.

[FRANK *searches* BASQUE'*s pockets.*]

FRANK:
What is it, Basque?

BASQUE:
A note.

FRANK:
I *know* a note.

BASQUE:
Somebody came for you. Try that back pocket.

FRANK:
What is this note?

BASQUE:
They put you on the docket.
Your case comes up today. The likelihood . . .
That tickles. No, no, keep going, that feels good.

FRANK:
Yes, yes, the *likelihood* . . .

BASQUE:
They're gonna bust you.

[*Getting turned on*]

A little lower. No, more left. There . . .

FRANK:
Must you?

BASQUE:
So maybe we should scram. Let's blow this burg.

[FRANK *sits on the trunk, weighing* BASQUE *down.*]

FRANK:

For what? So life, that heartless dramaturg,
Can plot another pitiless reversal?
Can wring my soul once more with no rehearsal?
Where would I go? I thought her tied to me.

BASQUE [*groaning under the pressure*]:
Monsieur . . .

FRANK:

                    And all this time she's lied to me!

[BASQUE *sinks gradually.*]

BASQUE:
But hey—ya know—this case—you still might win it . . .

[ELIANTE *enters.*]

ELIANTE:
Frank, may I speak to you for just a minute?

[BASQUE *exits with baggage and trunk.*]

FRANK:
Madame, thank God you're here. You've come in time
To right a wrong amounting to a crime.

ELIANTE:
You're right, you're right. I merit reprimanding.
My ardor stemmed from a misunderstanding.

FRANK:
To lead me on like that. Misguide me so.

ELIANTE:
I'm guilty, yes, but Frank—I didn't know!

FRANK:
Come down and look, you gods! To think a woman
So blessed with grace could be so base—inhuman . . .

ELIANTE:
It's true.

FRANK:
      And this same woman . . .

ELIANTE:
                      Me!

FRANK:
                            Whose name
I cannot even bring my lips to frame.

ELIANTE:
Oh, say it!

FRANK:
   No!

ELIANTE:
      Eliante!

FRANK:
           I'm too disgusted!

ELIANTE:
I couldn't help myself.

FRANK:
              She whom I trusted,
Who'd given me a vision of a world
Of love . . . !

ELIANTE:
      I'm sorry!

FRANK:

                Might as well have hurled
That vision in the mud with all her lies!

ELIANTE:

I never lied, not once!

FRANK:

                Desynchronize
The sun! Cast earth out of its polished groove,
I'd not be less astonished, or more moved!

ELIANTE:

Oh, Frank . . .

FRANK:

         And that's where you come in.

ELIANTE:

                      Who, I, sir?

FRANK:

You're good and kind. You're nice. What would be nicer
Than help redress this wrong?

ELIANTE:

                Yes.

FRANK:

                  Blunt this knife.

ELIANTE:

Yes.

FRANK:

   Show that there's some justice in this life.

ELIANTE:

Anything! Yes! I'll do it!

FRANK:

Be my wife.

ELIANTE:

I what?

FRANK:

Yes, yes, I know that as a match
There's not a single solitary patch
Of common ground between or even near us.
Hot sex right out of Sweden wouldn't endear us.
We're not a tango, much less *valse brillante,*
But will you marry me . . . um . . . ?

ELIANTE:

Eliante.

FRANK:

. . . Eliante?
Your silence must mean yes, or am I guessing?

ELIANTE:

Question: which wrong, again, am I redressing?

FRANK:

Your relative's, whose name I won't pronounce.
Celimene. Just imagine when we flounce
In here and say, right to her face, "We're married."
That ought to put her in her place. What varied
Emotions—jealousy, joy, rage, regret—
Will wrack her humbled heart! You want to bet
She'll cry?

ELIANTE:

Who wouldn't?

FRANK:

Look at that. You're weeping.

ELIANTE:
I don't know WHY!

FRANK:

                    And, in each other's keeping,
Who knows but that we might begin to love?
Calling each other darling, pumpkin, dove,
We might transcend our natural vanilla.
Perhaps we'll rent a quaint old Tuscan villa
And one day, gathering blooms, I take you in my arms . . .

[FRANK *takes* ELIANTE *in his arms.*]

Abruptly conscious of your female charms.
I can't! I can't! Oh, yes I can. I swallow.
We sink down to the fertile earth. We wallow
A while. A *long* while.

ELIANTE:
                    Is it good?

FRANK:

                                It's *good.*
I realize I've never understood
Your power, your infinite magnificence
And settling down with dismal diffidence
We live our lives in peace approaching Zen—
Then die upon a peak in Darièn!

ELIANTE:
I love you, Frank.

FRANK:
                    I love you, Celimene.
So kick the tires and think. It's in your power.
I'll come back for your answer in an hour.

ARSINOÉ [*from offstage*]:
Frank! *Frank!* What's keeping you?

FRANK:

I'm on my way!

[FRANK *exits as* CELIMENE *enters.*]

CELIMENE:
Was that just Frank?

ELIANTE:

Yes.

CELIMENE:

With Arsinoé?
So mocked, I hope, she's moving to Crimea.
Where were they going?

ELIANTE:

I have no idea.

CELIMENE:
Are you all right?

ELIANTE:

Um.

CELIMENE:

You look discomposed.

ELIANTE:
Ummm.

CELIMENE:

Well, thank God for Frank.

ELIANTE:

He just proposed.

CELIMENE:

He's helping with my . . . What?

ELIANTE:

He just proposed.
Asked me to marry him. Popped the top question.

CELIMENE:

This wasn't simply power of suggestion?
He dropped the word, you took it as a bid?
"Marriage," he said, you said, "I do"—?

ELIANTE:

He *did*.
He asked. My *name* he couldn't quite remember,
But—"*Be my wife*," he said. He's no dissembler.
You know that.

CELIMENE:

But . . .

ELIANTE:

Ask *him*.

CELIMENE:

Is this a joke?

ELIANTE:

No.

CELIMENE:

But . . .

ELIANTE:

But *what*?

CELIMENE:

Well, when we two last spoke
I indicated he and *I* might hook up.

ELIANTE:

I guess he's changed his mind.

CELIMENE:

                                So you cook up
A scheme to steal my beau away from me?

ELIANTE:

Your *beau*? You should have heard the calumny!
Not that he stinted on my own defects.
He hinted that not even Swedish sex
(Whatever that is) makes us plausible.

CELIMENE:

The River Sex is always crossable.

ELIANTE:

He might as well have asked a French gorilla.
But then he said we'd rent a Tuscan villa . . .

CELIMENE:

Wait. *Wait* . . .

ELIANTE:

                        And one day while we're gathering blooms . . .

CELIMENE:

Your gazes meet?

ELIANTE:

                        . . . a wanton flame consumes
Him. Sweeping me into his arms . . .

CELIMENE:

                                        You swoon
Down to the ground like quivering, juicy spoons?

ELIANTE:

We sink down to the fertile earth and *wallow.*

CELIMENE:
It's good?

ELIANTE:
       It's *good*. We're Daphne and Apollo,
Leda and Zeus, we are Persephone
And Hades! Frank's had an epiphany,
You see.

CELIMENE:
     I see. Before, he was deluded?

ELIANTE:
My infinite magnificence intruded.

CELIMENE:
Ah-ha. So you're in Tuscany, and then—?

ELIANTE:
We end up in some place called Darièn.

CELIMENE:
Connecticut?!

ELIANTE:
       He wants a quick reply.
What should I say?

CELIMENE:
       Maybe *"Die, bastard, die!"*—?

ELIANTE:
This *is* my lover.

CELIMENE:
       Lover? He's a *hater.*

ELIANTE:
He said you'd cry.

CELIMENE:

Oh, I'll save that for later.
But *why* ... ?

ELIANTE:

Philinte's the one who raised this hell.
First telling Frank you loved him (LOL)
And then, to bang a rivet in the coffin,
He told you Frank's some kind of royal dauphin.

CELIMENE:
But ...

ELIANTE:

Bastard cousin, I forget.

CELIMENE:

So he ...

ELIANTE:
The whole thing was a lie from A to Z.
Including (and you don't need twenty guesses)
Philinte's reputed bent for sky-blue dresses.

[PHILINTE *enters in a sky-blue gown, wearing a crown and carrying a scepter.*]

PHILINTE:
Make way, my people! All you rabble, move!
I'm sorry, can you point me to the Louv'?

CELIMENE:
Philinte, what is this? Joviality?

PHILINTE:
I've merged appearance and reality.
If people want to take on faith this line

I play a Habsburg when I'm home, then fine!
This city's so shot through with fraudulence
I'll match illusion to its audience.
I'll show their narrative's no empty crock.
I'll wear a fucking sky-blue frock.
All right, I spread a minuscule canard.
I'm hoisting Paris with its own petard!
I was a fool—a dupe, until today.
But now I see the lies that underlay
The social structure I depended on.
I was so good. I was a paragon . . .

[PHILINTE *digs out a handkerchief and blows his nose.*]

I was an angel, sweet as Polish toffee.

[DUBOIS *enters.*]

DUBOIS:
You want anything here?

CELIMENE:
                              Coffee. Coffee.

[DUBOIS *exits.*]

PHILINTE:
Now look—just look where all that goodness got me.

CELIMENE:
Philinte . . .

PHILINTE:
                  Life never gives us what we want.
Until today I thought I'd wed Eliante.

I guess it's not to be. That hope's a specter.
I'm in sateen and carrying a scepter!

[PHILINTE *is overcome.*]

CELIMENE:
Well, thank you for the mad scene. Boo hoo hoo.
You're clean. I'm asking, is it true-hoo-hoo
That Frank is not King Lou—(watch out, you're dribbling)

PHILINTE:
Thank you.

CELIMENE:
                  —that Frank is not King Louis's sibling?

PHILINTE:
It's true.

CELIMENE:
             It's true that *what*?

PHILINTE:
                              He's not.

CELIMENE:
                                        In short,
Frank's succor will mean zip to me in court.

PHILINTE:
You see? It's not that truth is multiple.
The problem is, we're all so gullible!

CELIMENE:
Can we please drop epistemology?
My problem's that, without apology,
Life is about to add me to the poor.
And not the ones in spirit. The real *pure* poor.

You know—those kind folks who sweep up manure
In front of our less plutocratic hovels?
That will be me. If I can raise a shovel.

PHILINTE:
I think—

CELIMENE:
        Could you please go powder your nose?

[PHILINTE *retreats to the corner.*]

Cuz, what would *you* do if we were transposed?

ELIANTE:
Temp job?

CELIMENE:
        The perils of Celimene. Stay tuned.

[DUBOIS *enters, followed by* CLITANDER, ACASTE, *and* ORONTE.]

DUBOIS:
Your hapless beaus!

[DUBOIS *throws himself into a chair and opens up a newspaper.*]

ORONTE:
           I take it you've communed
And reached a verdict who's to be your mate?

CLITANDER:
You've bounced between us long enough. A date
Is what we seek. No, no, please don't implore us.

CELIMENE:
I understand your pique, Monsieur Clitoris . . .

CLITANDER:
Tander.

CELIMENE:
      It's all so quick, you see, I'm dazed.

CLITANDER:
Quick? Two long years of chat and canapés?

ORONTE:
You must decide.

CELIMENE:
      So—marry, then, or burn.

ORONTE:
Indeed. Acaste?

ACASTE:
      I'm sorry. It's my turn?
Then—I agree. Whatever he said.

DUBOIS:
      Moron!

CELIMENE:
Well, gentlemen. I certainly could pour on
The charm, attempting to equivocate,
Or sidestep, trying to delay the date.
Would anyone like drinks? Some tea, or brandy?

ORONTE:
Madam . . .

CELIMENE:
      In fact, I have my judgment handy.
I know which one of you 's he. Have no fear.

ORONTE:
Name him, madame, or we'll be here all year!

ACASTE:
Well, in my heart I know that I am he
Because what *you* seek is stupidity.
A dupe to keep around the house, an idiot,
A dolt like me who's basically illiterate.
Someone invisible, who'll chew a ball
And settle for some kibble down the hall.
What fool would try to outshine Celimene?
He's bound to wind up an embellishment
To her incomparable élan and wit,
Her supersonic fame. I must admit,
I doubt I'm dense *enough,* but hell, I'm game.
I'll call her bluff and say that dupe is me
Just on the basis of . . .

[ACASTE *forgets what he was going to say.*]

CELIMENE:
                              Stu*pid* . . . ?

ACASTE:
                                        . . . stupidity.

ORONTE:
Wrong! I'm her choice because the fact remains
Her case necessitates a mate with *brains.*
You'd saddle Celimene with ignorami?

ACASTE:
It's true.

ORONTE:
           Why, from the moment I first came I
Knew. Her smart house a nest of indolence?
A partner who's possessed of *influence,*
That's what she wants—who can do something for her

Besides relieve himself in bowls and bore her.
A spouse with *nous*. Gray matter. High IQ.
I ask: does that sound like a man like you?

ACASTE:
No.

ORONTE:
　　　I'm alert, I'm quick, not diffident.
So what's the difference if I'm impotent?

ACASTE:
That's true.

ORONTE:
　　　　　I've conversation. I can *speak*.
I'll chant Euripides to her in Greek
While curled beside her like some literate fetus
And we from time to time attempt coitus.

DUBOIS:
Eeuww!

ACASTE:
All right. I may not win on ignorance.
But I'll match any man for impotence!

CLITANDER:
You're both wrong. I'm the man for this bewitcher.
I'm stupid *and* connected—and I'm richer.
Hasn't she made it clear she can be bought?
Well, with my mistress she will lack for naught.
I'll alternate—from her to Mistress Jiggly.
Oh, no, there'll be no rest for Mister Wiggly.
And as for impotence? Extraneous!
I am a *rock*. Just . . . instantaneous.
In time she'll bear a quota of young brats

And I'll abandon her to bridge and cats
So I can tend my life's delicious job:
Women, packed ass to tit like shish kebab.

ORONTE:
Well, there you have us, madam. Each appealing—

DUBOIS:
Whoa, yeah.

ORONTE:
        . . . in his own way. You see us kneeling.

[ORONTE *and* CLITANDER *kneel.*]

Kneel *down.*

ACASTE:
        I'm sorry.

CLITANDER:
                Well, you've heard our pitch.
Your question isn't *whether* now, but *which.*

[FRANK *enters with* ARSINOÉ.]

FRANK:
Up on your feet, you fungi. Save your knee joints.

[ORONTE *produces a document.*]

ORONTE:
Regard this paper, sir. On every point
Of my complaint the court has found against you.
As a result of which it has dispensed you
Penalties: first, one hundred thousand francs.

FRANK:
I've none to pay.

ORONTE:

           And banishment.

FRANK:

                         My thanks.
If saying a poem is shit makes me a baddie
I'll put on skins and move to Cincinnati.

ELIANTE:
But it's not over, Frank! You can appeal!

FRANK:
I wouldn't dream of begging for repeal.

ORONTE:
Madame, would you do like the court, and sever
This hanger-on from you, and here, forever?

FRANK:
The irony is that, for your protection,
It's *she* for whom you'll soon demand ejection.
Why? Letters!

[FRANK *produces them.*]

           Courtesy of . . . I won't say.

CELIMENE:
You needn't bother. Thanks, Arsinoé.

ARSINOÉ:
You stand too high, though, in my estimation
For me to dream that such abominations
Could flow from your so diplomatic pen.
Such vicious libels from our Celimene?

Such ridicule, such scurrilous aspersions?
Such filthy, low, erotical diversions?

ORONTE, ACASTE, AND CLITANDER:
Read them, read them!

FRANK [*reading*]:
       Fine. *"Darling"*—and I quote—
"God, how I long for you. Since last I wrote—
 Only two hours, which seems eternity,
 Kiss kiss kiss kiss—the mere uncertainty
 Of seeing you till night has driven me mad."
Not only filth, but trite. The prose is bad . . .

ORONTE, ACASTE, AND CLITANDER:
Go on!

FRANK:
   "I write this half-nude in my boudoir,
Thinking about our . . ." Something. Rhymes with *"boudoir"* . . .

CLITANDER, ACASTE, AND ORONTE:
Go on, go on!

FRANK:
    "What can intrude on our
Felicity when once we two are snuggling,
I cuddled by your side and you here, struggling . . ."
Enough.

[CLITANDER, ACASTE, *and* ORONTE *protest.*]

  What judge, what spouse, would not indict that?

CELIMENE:
There's only one small hitch: I didn't write that.

FRANK:
Oh, that excuse. Please. Tell it on the stand.

CELIMENE:
That note's to me, and in my cousin's hand.

CLITANDER, ACASTE, AND ORONTE:
Eliante!?

FRANK:
Yes, but . . .

CELIMENE:
You may approach the bench.

FRANK:
"I long for you . . ."?

CELIMENE:
It's girltalk.

FRANK:
"Kiss kiss kiss"?

CELIMENE:
We're French.

FRANK:
"Me, struggling"? Yes—the bacchanalian grovel!

CELIMENE:
Read.

FRANK:
"Struggling . . . with this new Italian novel . . ."

CELIMENE:
We read in bed. Now, Mr. Clairvoyant,
Check out the signature.

FRANK:
"Your own Eliante . . ."

CELIMENE:
So much for my "erotical diversions."

FRANK:
Well, fine. Let's see if this makes an incursion
On your good cheer.

[*Reading from another letter*]

"*My angel*" (underscored)
"*Would you were in this bed with me, <u>milord</u>,*
 To kiss and talk because I'm bored, bored, bored.
 And why? A visit from our friend Clitander,
 A cat who spreads his deadly dulling dander
 On every surface, though at least old Linus
 Does not insert a thumb into his sinus
 And from those tropic tufts of nostril hair
 Elicit gummy bits to flick at chairs . . ."

CLITANDER:
Enough, Monsieur!

FRANK:
                    You think she didn't mean it?

ACASTE:
I know Clitander does that, though. I've seen it.

FRANK:
Ah, yes, the bright Marquis. You get a mention.

ACASTE:
A compliment?

FRANK:
                    No doubt that's her intention.

[Reading from the letter]

"Acaste was here and gave me quite a lift
  Displaying his inimitable gift . . ."

ACASTE:
My singing?

FRANK:
                    ". . . leaning out the third-floor casement
And spitting, making puddles by the basement
That spell his name."

ORONTE:
                    I've seen him do it.

FRANK:
"At which he summons everyone to view it.
  The simpleton will spit like that for hours."

ACASTE:
I have to say, that is one of my powers.

FRANK:
"He makes me long for Nero and his fiddle.
  At least the house is fireproof, with its moat of spittle."

ACASTE:
How dare she call me simple! That's a slur!

ORONTE:
You've used the word yourself.

ACASTE:
                    I can, not her!

FRANK:
And you, Monsieur Boronte, complete our tour.

[Reading from another letter]

From last week, to her unnamed paramour.
"My angel, you'd be jealous if you saw me,
  But with no cause. How all men under-awe me
  Especially that worm—colon—Oronte."
  (She even got your name wrong.) *"The Worm flaunts*
  His sleep-inducing poems, and hopes to conquer.
  Would he could subjugate that purple honker."
There's more of similar color.

[ORONTE grabs the letter away.]

                              I'll refrain.
And finally, to paint her full disdain:

[Reading from another letter]

"You see, beloved, how I waste my arts
  On the unworthy, while unearthly hearts
  Like ours must walk in shadow down the glen.
  Each word here is a kiss from this, my pen.
  You've all my love forever, Celimene."

CLITANDER:
Well, well, madame. Behold your character.
I have no doubt what some fine barrister
Will call it in your trial once these are scanned.
And trust me, I'll be up there on the stand.

ACASTE:
Me, too. God *damn* it, but you take the palm.
All right, I'm simple. Yes! But I was *calm*!
Now look at me! I'm flushed, I'm faint, I'm flitting.
And may I ask what is so wrong with *spitting*?

ORONTE:
I never thought, madame, you'd use me thus.
And all the psalms I wrote (to you, to us)
You turn into the ravings of your dupe,
The self-delusions of some nincompoop?

DUBOIS:
That's right.

ORONTE:
                    I'll see you ruined. I'll see you flayed
And unto death you'll rue this game you played.
No, please don't try to beg. No words can salve me.
I hereby name your sentence: *you can't have me.*
The lack of me—and *this* [*he points to his wart*]—is your duress.

[*To* FRANK]

So take her, sir. I wish you both success.

CELIMENE:
Well, sir, what now? Finish, since you're so peeved.

FRANK:
Was ever woman such flint, or man so grieved?
Now see with what dispatch we two have flit
From apathy to bliss to bitter split.
With much confused, and still confusing, fusion
In one thin day we've summed up love's delusion.

ARSINOÉ:
Poor Celimene. Oh, dear, you look so shaken.
Why shouldn't you be? Your darling Frank is taken.

[ARSINOÉ *takes his arm.*]

FRANK:
I am?

ARSINOÉ:

Now you have me you needn't pine.

[ELIANTE *takes* FRANK'*s arm and pulls him away.*]

ELIANTE:
Excuse me, madam, but this man is mine.

ARSINOÉ:
Yours?

ELIANTE:

That's my property on which you're treading.
But I'll be sure to ask you to the wedding.

ARSINOÉ:
The wedding? Why, we're bound with brassy chains.

FRANK [*to* ARSINOÉ]:
Madam, I thank you for your many pains.
But how could I entrust my soul or body
To any woman who could be so shoddy,
So abhorrent, so desperate to ascend,
As to betray like this her own best friend?
No, no, it isn't right, nor is it just.
I'm not the man who's made to sate your lust.

ARSINOÉ:
Who said you were? Who said I wanted sating?
Well you, monsieur, a master-class in hating,
Have met your misanthropic equal now.
Call me a reprobate. Call me a cow.

DUBOIS:
You cow!

ARSINOÉ:

      I swear here an eternal oath
That I shall mete out justice to you both!
I'll have Her Royal Highness intervene!

[PHILINTE *steps forward.*]

DUBOIS:
All rise and bow! Her Majesty the Queen!

ALL:
Your Majesty!

[CLITANDER, ACASTE, ORONTE, *and* ARSINOÉ *bow and stay that way, faces to the floor.*]

PHILINTE [*as* QUEEN]:

      I have been privy—*don't move!*—
To your proceedings here. Now it behooves
Me, as a queen, to speak. I find it vile.

CLITANDER:
Yes, Lady. She—

PHILINTE [*as* QUEEN]:

      Not Celimene. Whose trial
In my meek judgment is a travesty.
Or don't you think so?

CLITANDER, ACASTE, ORONTE, AND ARSINOÉ:

      Yes, Your Majesty.

PHILINTE [*as* QUEEN]:
I mean you monsters from the Grand Guignol.
Now give back Celimene those notes you stole.

[ARSINOÉ, *face to floor, gives the notes to* CELIMENE.]

Well, then. It seems that there's no evidence.
So, given that fact—and out of deference
To me—you will not only stop this action,
Arsinoé, you'll print a full retraction
Of all the calumnies you've spread about—
And sign it, too, although your name casts doubt
On every phoneme your mandibles utter.
Now where's *the Worm*?

ORONTE:
                              Here.

PHILINTE [*as* QUEEN]:
                                        You, Boronte, will stutter
Retractions of your own down at the courts.
I want to see a verdict that comports
With justice. Namely: Frank exonerated
And, just to show that you've corroborated,
You will pay Frank the hundred thousand fine—
Nor ever, *ever* write another line.
And lose the wart. There! Justice has been meted.
And one last word, now evil has been cheated:
I wasn't here.

ALL:
            No, Majesty.

PHILINTE:
                    Now beat it!

[CLITANDER, ACASTE, ORONTE, and ARSINOÉ exit, still bent at the waist. PHILINTE and DUBOIS exit another way.]

ELIANTE:
Well, it's been quite a day—and it's not through.
Amidst its chaos I learned this is true:
I'm not your soul mate, Frank. No, I release you.
I couldn't bear to see that serpent seize you,
And spoke less out of love than out of spite.
Though love was there.

FRANK:
                         Madame, you have done right,
As always, being the very soul of kindness.
I also have a truth, which in the blindness
And fury of event you failed to see.
I always knew you weren't the one for me.
No, you're Philinte's. He's sane—or was. He's steady.
Besides—I am a married man already.

ELIANTE:
You're married?

FRANK:
                         Yes, God help me. Wed to her.
We're like those double stars whose auras blur.
And though I know that it's society
That's made her this, that notoriety
Has spoiled her virtue, taken off her bloom—
She's still a traitress.

CELIMENE:
                         Traitress, sir, to whom?

FRANK:
To me! To me! The passion in those letters?

CELIMENE:
I didn't know you.

FRANK:

Who was their begetter?
You wrote *one day* after your husband's death—

[*Reading a letter*]

"*My love, you're everything to me. You're breath
And life and love. You are death's enemy.*"
I, love a woman with a memory
As short as that?

ELIANTE:

All right, she's not a saint . . .

CELIMENE:
No, stop, Eliante. He has a just complaint.
My acts he justifiably finds filthy.
But it's not I who in my heart is guilty—
It's Celimene as I may once have been.
Not to be what I once was—that's my sin.
Yes, were he here, my late beloved spouse
Would wail the state of his beloved house
And how his Celimene has had to shift.
But he's not here. Among his many gifts
Not being, unfortunately, resurrection.
So here I stand beyond Alceste's detection.
See me as I am. Imperfect. Uncouth.
And since you're so devoted to the truth
I'll say now what I couldn't when you asked me:
I love you. I love you. Now you've unmasked me.
As no man has, you've put me to the test.
A small correction: no man since Alceste.

You have what he had, now gone out of fashion:
Ultra-true, unadulterated passion.

[FRANK *holds up the letters.*]

FRANK:
And *this* man? I suppose he was a ruse?

CELIMENE:
I won't apologize. I've no excuse.
Though you might ask how notes meant for some darling
Were found in my possession. Sir, you're snarling.

FRANK:
Lie to me. Lie. Swear this affair's at rest.

CELIMENE:
Monsieur, I wrote those letters to Alceste.

FRANK:
You what . . . ?

CELIMENE:
                He sparked this lengthy correspondence
By being lost at sea. In my despondence
I wrote to him. Would he could write to me.

FRANK:
Then write to him no longer. I am he.

[FRANK *puts on a pair of glasses, revealing himself. There is general amazement.*]

ALCESTE:
Two years abandoned on a rocky islet—
Two years with you, as ever, my sole pilot,
Then rescued, having heard of your new fame

As hostess and the blots upon your name,
I came to verify these rumored lovers—
Bitter in truth, with bitterness my cover.
What wonder then to find you, if notorious,
So much the same: resilient, brilliant, glorious.
A million women couldn't match you, Sal.
Forgive the ruses of your long-lost pal.
I venerate, I worship, I adore you.
Well, Sally? Well?

CELIMENE:

I have some letters for you.

[CELIMENE *throws herself into his arms.*]

Alceste . . . !

ALCESTE:

So you don't mind my sea of lies?

CELIMENE:
You think I didn't see through your disguise?
I may be older but I've not gone blind.
I had you pegged from—

ALCESTE:

When?

CELIMENE:

Oh . . . never mind.

ALCESTE:
Eliante—will *you* forgive me?

ELIANTE:

Are you kidding?
The man who forced me to put down my knitting?
What now, though, now that all my life's awry?

ALCESTE:
Take up a husband. I know just the guy.

ELIANTE:
You mean Philinte?

ALCESTE:
                    I know you can't abide him.
But after today, don't speak until you've tried him.
And here's the future groom now, newly dressed.

[PHILINTE *enters, as himself again.*]

PHILINTE:
What did I miss?

ALCESTE:
                    Oh, nothing.

PHILINTE:
                              Christ! *Alceste!*

CELIMENE:
The man himself, in all his former glory.

PHILINTE:
But what . . . ? But how . . . ?

ALCESTE:
                              A complicated story.

[BASQUE *enters, carrying a clinking, bulging sack.*]

BASQUE:
Monsieur—some guy just left this bag.

ALCESTE:
                              Wow. Thanks.

BASQUE:
I counted it. A hundred thousand francs.
You know what else? I swear you're gonna grin.
Her butler?—"Canapé?"—'s my long-lost twin!

ALL:
No!

BASQUE:
Yeah! At birth we two got separated.
I got the dreck and he got decorated.

CELIMENE:
Well, send him in!

BASQUE:
Uh . . . Yeah . . . That could be tricky.
He's making some hors d'oeuvres. His hands are sticky.

[BASQUE *exits.*]

ALCESTE:
Sally—let's run.

CELIMENE:
What?

ALCESTE:
Run. Let's run away.
There's nothing keeping us. Why should we stay
To see ourselves grow old in this gray city?
The world out there's still young, and what a pity
To miss its endless interweaving track.

CELIMENE:
You want to leave? But, Al, you just got back!

ALCESTE:
And you've been cooped up here. Would you be cheated?
This bag's the world. Let's spend till it's depleted.

CELIMENE:
You've *seen* the world.

ALCESTE:

But not with you. With Sally.
Your eyes will metamorphose every alley
Into a pilgrim's pathway paved with gold,
Each valley to a vale . . .

CELIMENE:

Alceste—I'm sold.

[ALCESTE *and* CELIMENE *bolt out of the room, shouting "Good-bye! Good-bye!" as* DUBOIS *enters, munching hors d'oeuvres from a tray of canapés.*]

ELIANTE:
We'll have to mind this big old house, I guess.

PHILINTE:
Eliante . . .

ELIANTE:

I would. I do. The answer's YES!

[*They share a small kiss.*]

PHILINTE:
What happened?

ELIANTE:

Well . . . I think it was the dress!

[PHILINTE *bends her over in a passionate kiss.*]

DUBOIS:
YES!

[*CURTAIN.*]